■ A F T E R   T H E   L A W

A book series edited by John Brigham and Christine B. Harrington

GIGS

"Surround the place, I think I hear one of those rowdy jazzmen in there!"

GIGS

JAZZ AND THE CABARET LAWS IN NEW YORK CITY

■ PAUL CHEVIGNY

■ ROUTLEDGE   NEW YORK■LONDON

Published in 1991 by

Routledge
An imprint of Routledge, Chapman and Hall, Inc.
29 West 35th Street
New York, NY 10001

Published in Great Britain by

Routledge
11 New Fetter Lane
London EC4P 4EE

Library of Congress Cataloging-in-Publication Data

Chevigny, Paul, 1935–
    Gigs : Jazz and the cabaret laws in New York / Paul
Chevigny.
        p. cm.—(After the law)
    Includes bibliographical references and index.
    ISBN 0-415-90400-5
    1. Performing arts—New York (N.Y.)—History—20th century.
    2. New York (N.Y.)—Popular culture—History—20th century.
    3. Musicians—Legal status, laws, etc.—New York (N.Y.) 4. Music
halls (Variety theaters, cabarets, etc.)—Law and legislation—New
York (N.Y.) 5. Jazz—New York (N.Y.)—History and criticism.
    I. Title. II. Series.
PN2277.N5C515   1991
791'.09747'10904—dc20   91-17611
                                                            CIP

British Library Cataloguing in Publication Data

Chevigny, Paul, 1935–
    Gigs : music and the cabaret laws in New York.—
    (After the law)
    I. Title   II. Series.
    347.470378791

    ISBN 0-415-90400-5

I'd rather drink muddy water, sleep out in a hollow log,
I'd rather drink muddy water, Lord, sleep out in a
hollow log,
Than be up here in New York, treated like a dirty dog.

—Jack Teagarden

This book is dedicated to
Thelonious Monk, J. J. Johnson, Billie Holiday, Buell
Neidlinger
and all the other good musicians who had a problem with the
cabaret laws.

CONTENTS

ACKNOWLEDGMENTS

An enormous number of people and organizations have helped both to change the New York City cabaret laws and to produce this book. I want to remember as many of them here as I can, because their work has been so important to me and the City.

Musicians who helped are Warren Chiasson, Mark Morganelli, Carol Cass, Milt Hinton, John Carisi, Joel Forrester, Buell Neidlinger, Junior Mance, Barry Harris, David Amram, George Simon, Henry Threadgill, Carol Britto, Arnie Lawrence, Virginia Mayhew, Rebecca Franks, Peter Bernstein, James R. Belden, Lodi Carr, Peter LaRoca Sims, Bobby Sanabria, Ken McIntyre, Jack Walrath, Terry Pender and Tony Trischka.

Lawyers who worked on the case or helped with the book, or both, are Robert Campbell, Jeffrey Cylkowski, Peter LaRoca Sims again, Robert Bookman, Norman Marcus, Liza Dubrul, Elise Wagner, my colleagues Peggy Davis and Claudia Angelos, students in the Civil Rights Clinic at NYU Law School, and, of course, Justice David Saxe. My student research assistants Clarke Bruno and Ruth Singleton helped enormously on the book.

Club owners and others connected with the music business who helped are Paul Pines, Marvin and Monica Hughes, Mike and Pat Mikell, Phil Schaap, Janet Solesky, Stefan Bauer-Mengelberg, Mel Litoff, Art D'Lugoff, Paul Moore, Andy Lugris, Felice Kirby, Michael Dorf, Robert Appell, Gus Cualtas, Joseph Termini, Mike Cantarino and Judy Barnett.

Among the critics, journalists and students of the music who helped are Peter Watrous, Jon Pareles, Stuart Troup, David

Levy, now Director of the Corcoran Gallery, Dan Morgenstern, Nat Hentoff, Michael Cuscuna and Eric Samler.

Among the public officials who helped to understand or solve the problems are Deborah Silberstein, Bonnie Buch, Sylvia Deutsch, Barbara Fife, Peter Lempin, Eva Hanhardt, Councilmember Stanley Michels and especially Manhattan Borough President Ruth Messinger.

Those who helped me to think about the land-use problems are Fred Kent, Richard Sennett, William H. Whyte, Brian Ketcham, Sigurd Grava, the Natural Resources Defense Council and the Municipal Art Society. Daniel Queen gave expert advice on the problems of noise.

For essential research materials and facilities, I thank the Theater and Music Collections of the New York Public Library at Lincoln Center, and the Institute for Jazz Studies at Rutgers University, Newark, New Jersey.

My special thanks to the Associated Musicians of Greater New York, Local 802 of the American Federation of Musicians, and especially to my friends President John Glasel, Judy West and David Sheldon.

Many thanks for reading and criticising the manuscript to Christine Harrington, John Brigham, the Routledge staff and The Group, and again to Christine and John for urging me to write the book. And to Bell, who liked the idea of the case and loved the idea of the book, even when I was doubtful.

I was free to write much of the book in the summer of 1990 due to a generous grant from the Filomen D'Agostino and Max E. Greenberg Research Fund to the New York University School of Law. Thanks also to the Cummington Community of the Arts, where much of the draft was written, and to Antonio Frasconi for the use of his woodcut on the book jacket.

INTRODUCTION

This book is about rights and music, mostly jazz music. For more than sixty years, from 1926 until 1990, live music played in bars and restaurants in New York City was restricted by local regulations called collectively "the cabaret laws." Although we usually think of a cabaret as a place with a floor-show, the City extended the reach of its regulations even to restaurants with live music. The laws imposed a complex system of licensing combined with zoning restrictions on the neighborhoods where live music could be played; outside those neighborhoods where licensing was permitted, the laws allowed only background music, with a limit on the number and even the types of instruments that could be played. Despite minor amendments, the cabaret laws endured with astonishingly little change over that long period; they came to represent discrimination and degradation to the musicians who played in nightclubs. From time to time, musicians pressed for change in the laws; one of those times was in the 1980s.

During the period 1986 to 1990, the regulations were changed to permit live music to be played in restaurants and bars generally, requiring a licence only in the larger establishments. Although the change began through lobbying and political agitation by the musicians union, it came to center around a case that I pressed as a volunteer, helped by other lawyers, for the musicians and their union. The case attacked the regulations through the claim that they violated the musicians' freedom of expression.

1

Our case was successful, within the bounds of litigation; the court declared the regulations unconstitutional, leading to their nearly complete overhaul. Yet the case was not an obvious, much less inevitable candidate for success; my impression at the time I started work on it was that most lawyers who had heard about the case were predicting that it would fail. And so the change in the cabaret laws raises a classic problem in the politics of law: under what circumstances are assertions of rights through litigation successful?

One popular view pictures such victories as triumphs for an essentially autonomous body of rights. In this view, at least in the version popularly purveyed in the United States, the lawyer is cast as the hero; he is the "lone gun" who comes up with arguments, pitches them to the court, gets a written opinion and order and forces change on the world. The cabaret case was sometimes seen as such a story, and I was cast in the role of the lone gun. The Municipal Art Society awarded me a certificate of merit "for leading the victorious through long and often lonely legal battles to overturn the restrictive cabaret law," and the *New York Times* even wrote a little piece about me.[1]

Although I am not so modest that I am not flattered by these honors, I have to admit that there are some puzzling aspects to the "rights marshalled by the smart lawyer" story of socio-legal change. Set aside the question of why the lawyer, rather than the judge, is cast as the hero.[2] If the rights are really doing the work, why should any mere jurist be a hero in the piece at all? He would seem to be no more than the craftsperson who assembles the tools and uses them to get a result; it is the law that should be the hero in this scenario. The reason why the lawyer and the legal rights go together in this morality play, I think, is that any power that rights can mobilize, or that can be mobilized for them, is written out of the story. As in the Western movie, in which the hero can win against improbable odds if he has right on his side, so in this story the lone jurist armed with rights can triumph over intimidating power.

There is a contrasting account of law and legal change in

which, in its simplified version, power is everything. In this view, the conceptual structure of such rights as freedom of expression is so manipulable that it can take on meanings almost as needed, particularly in a situation like the cabaret case, where the previous law is not very well articulated. A change in the law to help musicians, or anyone else, occurs only when it is in the interest of dominant forces in society that change should occur. The lawyer's job, if he has one, is to see to it that officials do not overlook his client's case in the course of the change, and to expedite a change that is bound to occur by keeping the need for it before everyone's eyes through litigation, the press and every other means.

I am not prepared to accept either one of these caricatures—neither the "autonomous rights" nor the "manipulated rights" version—of the workings of law and legal change. There are, of course, much more subtle versions of both sorts of views, that try to take account of power, including the power of ideas. But the question remains: what does happen when, as in this case, rights are asserted successfully and a change in the law eventually issues? What forces bring about the change? And does the change in law make any concrete social difference, or is it merely formal, a change in rhetoric?

This book attempts to offer some answers in the case of the change in the New York City cabaret laws, through a fine-grained analysis at a local level of the cultural and social situation of vernacular music, particularly jazz, of the law concerning the music, and the politics and consequences of the change. It is worth mentioning that the case did not present a major break-through in constitutional law, nor result in any change in the principles of law. The case was, nevertheless, of some practical importance to musicians; the challenge to the cabaret laws was a matter of using existing concepts to get new, practical results, rather than one of a sea change in the law. That characteristic of the case is quite helpful for my study, because the absence of dramatic doctrinal change leaves us free to concentrate on what cultural and social change occurred, and why. Thus, the study focuses not so much on law alone as on law in society. In addition to constitutional rights, it draws on several bodies of law that affected the status of live music, including the labor laws and the regulatory system itself.

As applied to music, the cabaret laws were principally of symbolic value to those who enforced them; they expressed the view of the New York City lawmakers—rooted ultimately in racism as well as fear of bohemian mores—that vernacular music was not entitled to be treated with respect. Such an enforcement of status is characteristic of lawmaking about the arts; those who legislate voice their sense that one style is socially acceptable and that another is not, and by their acts make the discrimination come true. That is one reason why regulation attempting to control the content of artistic expression is often condemned legally as censorship. Even when a regulation can, for one reason or another, pass muster under the Constitution, the legislative impulse remains the same; the recent attack on the funding for the National Endowment for the Arts, for example, is an effort to assert such symbolic control.[3] In Joseph Gusfield's classic formulation, this sort of control "expresses the public worth of one subculture's norms relative to those of others, demonstrating which cultures have legitimacy and public domination. Accordingly it enhances the social status of groups carrying the affirmed culture and degrades groups carrying that which is condemned as deviant. . . ."[4] The cabaret laws, as we shall see, branded popular, especially jazz, music as deviant with great precision and for a very long time.

More broadly, local zoning regulations make such symbolic judgments for virtually all the functions of a city. Their very reason for being is to regulate land use according to the values and the tastes of those who plan for the city—they discriminate among neighborhoods and among uses for particular neighborhoods, according to class and functional differences. In New York City, for example, there are zones designated as C5, called "gilt-edged" commercial districts—like the shopping district on

Fifth Avenue in Midtown Manhattan—from which entertainment is supposed to be excluded.

Zoning and similar regulations typically differ from laws like Prohibition, which Gusfield selected as the *locus classicus* of symbolic legislation, because they are much more widely accepted and nearly invisible. People live under zoning and are for the most part scarcely aware of it. Zoning simply sets forth—represents—the character of the city and its neighborhoods. Even in cases where, if asked, people might object to some of the categorizations in the zoning regulations, they usually do not think about them. So it was for many years, in the zoning of music clubs; people did not expect the situation to be other than it was. Only as regulations become grossly out of keeping with the character of neighborhoods in a changing city do people experience them as harassing legislation of morality instead of "the way things are." Thus, it is worth noting that when the court struck down the restrictions on music clubs in 1988, musicians as well as journalists likened the action to the end of Prohibition.

For much of the time that the cabaret laws were in effect, jazz musicians experienced their lives as scuffling for a living, "on the outs" both musically and economically. These artists played a vital music, but they paid a price to be able to do it. And for most of those years, the cabaret laws both expressed and reinforced those attitudes from the City's side. The laws restricted where the music could be played, and at one time permitted only licensed musicians to play it, thus excluding some able musicians from New York clubs.

For many years, officers of the union, the American Federation of Musicians, shared some of the prejudices, including the racism and the dismissive attitude toward the music. As the Associated Musicians of Greater New York—Local 802 of the AFM—changed its views and took up the cause of jazz musicians against the cabaret laws, the social function of the clubs where the music was played was changing as well. The cabaret laws, still expressing a prejudice against the vernacular arts, failed to keep up with the social and cultural change in the music and the clubs.

Thus the union, itself somewhat altered, was the immediate catalyst for change in the regulations. Nevertheless, the City, through inertia and inveterate prejudice, seemed capable of resisting change indefinitely, relying on variations of arguments it had been using for generations. Even after our First Amendment case was successful, the City, through the City Planning Department, the Department of Consumer Affairs and the City Council, continued to resist the change by trying to pass "reform" zoning and licensing laws that were little altered from the originals.

The rights of expression of the musicians, together with their consciousness and the city government's consciousness—or lack of consciousness—of those rights, turned out to be important. For most of the sixty years of the regulations, neither jurists nor musicians thought much about the rights of "popular entertainers" at all. Although jazz musicians did not accept the way they were treated by social and political forces in New York City— a great many were then and still are infuriated by it—they had no clear notion of how the situation could be otherwise, except through a complete change of societal attitudes to the music. The acceptance of a well-defined right for musicians to express themselves as they pleased, in the forms that they choose, changed their own attitudes and the attitudes of government. Constitutional law supplied a framework for arguments against the existing system of zoning and licensing which otherwise were rather formless and powerless matters of opinion. The assertion of rights afforded a system of belief in which cultural change could be accepted, and provided a way—litigation— of organizing the change. Nevertheless, it remains true that acceptance of those rights finally made them work.

The results, perhaps to no one's surprise, lend little support to the formalistic "lonely battle" model of legal action. In the end the change in the law was effective only insofar as a number of social actors gave their consent. In the end, a cultural change, or rather an overdue legal and social change in the light of a long-term cultural change, combined with political and economic change to make possible a real alteration in status.

This book begins in Chapter One with a sketch of the musical and regulatory situation as it was just before the case began. The narrative then goes back in history to explain the place of all the institutional actors in the process of change. Chapter Two locates the musicians union, and particularly its New York branch, Local 802, in the context of the constraints on its organization. These included changing attitudes to live music and to organized labor, parallel changes in the labor laws, as well as class and social conflicts within the union itself that illuminate its reactions to the cabaret laws. Chapter Three considers the relation between jazz music and the clubs. Although this chapter traces a rough history of the clubs, showing how the music was developed, chiefly by black musicians and originally in illegal speakeasies, it does not pretend to be exhaustive. The story is concerned, however, with enduring patterns in the way the music is learned and played in the clubs, as well as the marginal economic status of the clubs and their social status as bohemian "joints." The developments reflect the changing place of the music, as it has been played less for dancing and has taken on more "respectability." Chapter Four traces the history of New York's regulations for nightclubs—under the misnomer of "cabarets"—showing how the regulations represented repressive attitudes toward jazz music, the people who played and sang it, and the places where it was played, resulting in a licensing system for both musicians and clubs. The chapter explains the complexity of the regulatory system, which joins licensing with zoning and other regulations, making change extremely difficult. Here, the influence of public opinion through the press appears; it will broaden in later chapters. Chapter Five describes the push for change in the eighties, with Local 802's lobbying effort to change the licensing system. This campaign illustrates a principal danger in a narrowly "legal" struggle—that it will be drawn into a drive for those gains that the political system is most likely to yield. For example, Local 802 began its campaign for a change in the licensing of clubs without taking into account the need for a parallel change in zoning policy, because there were city legislators ready to introduce an amendment to the licensing ordinance, but no one offering to change the zoning laws. Thus we encounter the invidious judgments underlying the zoning of nightclubs, together with the legal procedures for changes in zoning, made particularly cumbersome by attempts to decentralize city government. The problems of this chapter point directly to the lawsuit described in Chapter Six, which reflects changing attitudes toward affirmative civil rights litigation, as well as a shift in the treatment of "entertainment" under the First Amendment. The influence of the press upon the process had become enormous by this point in the story. One of the themes of Chapter Seven is that the results of a suit against a governmental body, however successful for the plaintiffs, do not take root without some acceptance by the defendants. The chapter recounts how the City acquiesced in part, while resisting in the large, in an effort to maintain governmental control and to preserve its moribund zoning aims. The result of the case was finally accepted because of a shift in administration and an economic downturn in the City. Chapter Eight considers the only really effective change—the one that took place in the lives of the musicians. The influence of increased legal liberty, it turns out, has been limited by the economic weakness of the clubs, as well as the marginal popularity of jazz music. The book concludes with reflections about the entire process: how complex and chancy it is to grapple with the social, economic and political forces of change, even at a local level, and how ambiguous are the results.

I make no systematic attempt to describe the City of New York itself, either as a political or a cultural entity, although some of its institutions—legal ones like the Uniform Land Use Review Procedure or cultural institutions like the jazz clubs—are treated in detail. I pause here to sketch some of the City's governmental institutions, chiefly so that the reader will be familiar with the terminology, and will not be dulled by the word salad and alphabet soup that is characteristic of talk about the particulars of government in the United States. The mayor is of course the chief executive officer of the City.[5] He appoints a number of commissioners, including those for the Fire, Police and Buildings Departments, as well as one responsible for administering licenses. The latter, at one time called the Commissioner of Licenses, was changed during the Lindsay Administration to become the Commissioner of Consumer Affairs, in an effort to change the emphasis of the job from enforcement and control to service to the public.

The City Council is the main legislative body, although during the period described in this book, its zoning powers were limited. Until 1990, final decision-making power for land-use planning was vested in the Board of Estimate, a body made up of the mayor, the president of the City Council, the comptroller and the presidents of the five boroughs. The City Planning Commission, using its staff in the City Planning Department, draws up the overall plan for land use in the City, including the designation of districts and the uses that are appropriate to them, through the Zoning Resolution, which has the force of law and was at that time subject to the approval of the Board of Estimate. There are also local Community Boards, as well as borough-wide boards, which have advisory powers concerning changes in zoning and decisions on particular building projects.

The fragmentation of functions implied by this profusion of commissioners, planners and legislators is central to an understanding of the difficulties that lie in the way of changes in regulations in the City, especially those that effect the use of land. Basic is a division between the zoning-planning function, which was at that time given to the City Planning Commission and the Board of Estimate, and the function of licensing businesses, which was and still is given to the Department of Consumer Affairs, under laws passed by the City Council. Thus every restaurant or bar that offered "entertainment" not only had to have a license to operate, but had to be located in a zone approved for entertainment.

As will be described in more detail in Chapters Five and Seven, restaurants and bars are permitted in all commercial zones in the City, while under the cabaret laws nightclubs were permitted only in certain commercial zones and in manufacturing districts. Thus it was not possible to obtain a "cabaret license" for a nightclub from the licensing authorities unless the place was located in one of the approved zones. Still more baroque regulatory variations were possible. In some zones where nightclubs were not ordinarily permitted, it was nevertheless possible to apply for a cabaret license if the applicant received a special permit from the Board of Standards and Appeals, a body made up of planners and engineers appointed by the mayor. In those zones, then, there was in effect a system of double licensing, by the Board as a zoning matter, as well as by the city licensing body. The double licensing process could be a daunting venture into a bureaucratic minefield, as we shall see in more detail in Chapter Seven.

New York City government became slightly simpler in 1990. The Board of Estimate was abolished in 1989, after a dramatic lawsuit attacked the structure of the Board, which favored the less-populous boroughs, through the "one person, one vote" rule under the Equal Protection clause of the Constitution.[6] Land-use planning is now centered in the City Council and the City Planning Commission. And of course, the regulation of music clubs—the subject of this book—has been changed.

As these bones take on flesh in the chapters of this book, the interrelation of the city government and other social and political forces will become more clear. The fact that this book is a study of political change at a local level, through local regulations, affords special dividends in the study of the symbolic power of the law. The discretion of the municipality in the expression of values through zoning is great, and the value judgments are often expressed with discrimination and subtlety; New York City, for example, set aside a "gilt-edged" commercial district that was closed to entertainment except in hotels. The details of zoning show what the mandarins of municipal planning care about, and just how and just when they will change what they care about. Social change described at this level of detail should make the City's institutions, and their history, familiar—and at the same time strange.

Because this book is about recent events in which I participated and came to know many of the actors, it has some restrictions that it would not have if it were fictional, or if I were an outsider. I have not, for the most part, tried to characterize people involved in the events, nor talked about my opinions of their actions, except in a few cases where I am in an outright and obvious adversarial position. The reader often must draw her own conclusions from the circumstances of the narrative. To some extent, I am following a long-standing custom in the music business. For example, I am rarely critical of a club or its owner, even if I have heard critical reports, because a club is, after all, still a place for musicians to work, even if the boss is a thief or a closet Lawrence Welk fan. And I do not make invidious comparisons among the work of musicians. I have listened to the work of every musician discussed in these pages, and I think all of it is at least good and competent, even though the work of some musicians is much more to my taste than that of others.

Many of the musicians and the clubs described here are not famous or financially successful; indeed, it is those who are marginal who are most likely to be affected by the legal changes described here. Thus some of my information may prove to have been fugitive. Some clubs described here may be out of business by the time this is published, and some musicians may have left New York or even have gone into another line of work.

I use the term "vernacular music" to connote collectively all the forms of music with a popular base that are played in the New York clubs, in preference to another phrase, because it conveys a sense of the attitude of class superiority that the City has often exhibited toward the music, and because an alternative term like "popular music" is often used to describe only commercialized forms of music. Nevertheless, the book concentrates on jazz. It might have been written with a slant toward rock, or more lately toward blues bars, or toward the tradition of ballad singing that has been developed in New York clubs. Jazz, however, as I noted at the outset of this introduction, has the longest pedigree, going all the way back to the inception of the cabaret laws in 1926, and is, as one deputy mayor said, the "signature music" for the New York clubs.

Ultimately the best reason for concentrating on jazz is that it is the music I know most about. I have been listening to it in myriad New York clubs for forty years; I recognise the styles and understand the arguments about them much better than I do with other music. It is, when all is said and done, the reason that I came to grips with the social, political and legal problems that are the stuff of this book.

CHAPTER I

PRELUDE

My wife, Bell, and I got to know Marvin and Monica Hughes many years ago when our children went to the same school. We all lived on the Upper West Side of Manhattan, where we commiserated from time to time about the cost of housing. The Hugheses had a nice cooperative apartment, which they were able to sell in the mind-boggling real estate boom beginning at the end of the seventies, to move to Riverdale in the Bronx. They kept one foot in Manhattan by realizing their long-standing dream of opening a cafe. Coming from a European musical family, Monica subscribed to a cafe tradition including good food, coffee and the arts; Marvin dreamed of a jazz club. They contrived to combine the two.

The Burgundy Cafe opened in 1982 on Amsterdam Avenue, north of 82nd Street. Although very small, the cafe was cleverly designed to hold a few dozen people, with a bar in the middle, and behind it a little mezzanine. The food was indeed good, and every month they exhibited the work of a different artist on the walls. In her affidavit in the musicians' case against the City's cabaret laws, Monica told the story:

> Shortly after the Burgundy opened, we started having music, at first at brunch on weekends, and then in the evenings on weekends. We have used both classical and jazz musicians, although we have tended to emphasize jazz. Because the Burgundy is quite small, we have never used a group larger than a trio.

During 1983, we gradually expanded our music, until we had musicians playing most nights of the week. At that time we had no piano, and we used all sorts of small combinations, particularly saxophone and bass. We employed singers with interesting trio and duet groups. We had marvelously talented musicians playing original music using instruments that I later learned were illegal under the cabaret laws. For example, noted saxophonists such as Ricky Ford, Sonny Fortune, Lee Konitz and Ken McIntyre performed at the Burgundy.

In addition, on many Wednesday evenings during 1984, Mark Morganelli played trumpet and flugelhorn, in a duet with a guitar or a vibraphone. Warren Chiasson played vibraphone on at least one occasion. Both men are excellent, creative musicians, who played music that we liked.[1]

One night Ricky Ford, whose trademark was then a sport jacket with painted lapels, and a correspondingly confident and colorful command of the saxophone, played with the great bassist Reggie Workman. Although saxophone and bass fiddle might seem an odd combination, the Burgundy was so small that the balance was good. There was no microphone; the audience sat right next to the woody pulse of Workman's instrument. The two men were, as the expression is, wailing. During a break between sets, I said the music was too good to miss, and I had to go home to get my wife. In a New York bar, such a proposition is apparently viewed as improbable, and everyone was amused when I actually did bring Bell back for the next set. Whenever he recognized me after that, Reggie Workman identified me as the guy who thought the music was so good he went home to get his wife.

Thus the Burgundy was the realization of a dream of mine, just as it was of the Hugheses: a jazz club around the corner from my home, run by people whom I actually knew. The club developed a group of regulars, as coffee houses, bars and especially jazz clubs will, people who came often, knew one another at least to say hello, and enjoyed the music and the low-pressure atmosphere.

The Burgundy did get a piano, a handsome Baldwin grand that, unlike most club pianos, was actually kept in tune, so that players wanted to come to the place to get a chance to use it. But by 1985, horn players were increasingly rare. When I asked Monica what had happened to them, she said, "Would you believe it's illegal to have a saxophone in here?" lowering her voice as though she might still get a summons.

I didn't believe it. Literally. I thought someone must have been pulling her leg. She said I ought to call the musicians union, because she had heard that they were trying to do something about it. I first looked up the New York City cabaret-licensing ordinance, which did indeed say just what Monica claimed and more. It not only forbade percussion as well as typical jazz front-line instruments such as horns, but it restricted the number of musicians to three—a limitation the Hugheses had hardly noticed, because they could not accommodate more than a trio. The regulation twisted the cultural knife by allowing any sort of canned music.

> "Cabaret" Any room place or space in the city in which any musical entertainment, singing, dancing or other form of amusement is permitted in connection with the restaurant business or the business of directly or indirectly selling to the public food or drink, except eating or drinking places, which provide incidental musical entertainment, without dancing, either by mechanical devices, or by not more than three persons playing piano, organ, accordian [sic], guitar or any stringed instrument or by not more than one singer accompanied by himself or a person playing piano, organ, accordian, guitar or any stringed instrument.[2]

A "cabaret," into which The Burgundy was transformed, according to this legal definition, every time it employed a saxophone player, was by law required to get a license. The

Hugheses, having opened a restaurant and acquired a liquor license, were not about to slog through another licensing process. Monica doubted that their location was even eligible to get a cabaret license under the zoning laws. She was quite right, as I understood later; for that part of Amsterdam Avenue, they would have needed a special permit from the zoning authorities.[3] And so the Burgundy tried, like a lot of other places, to have something that would look to an inspector like the "incidental musical entertainment" specified in the regulation—something, that is, without horns or percussion.

I did call Local 802, the New York affiliate of the musicians union, and spoke to Judy West, the Public Relations Director. I vented my indignation and volunteered to help. Although she was pleased to get any help she could, Ms. West might have said to me what Gandhi, most of his life's work completed, is supposed to have said to his assassin: "You are late." By the spring of 1985, the union had been at work on the problem of the discrimination against horns and percussion in the "incidental music" exception for months. In a more general way, the union and its members had been grappling with the cabaret laws for more than a generation.

When a new administration, led by John Glasel, a former jazz trumpeter, had been elected in Local 802 in 1983, there was a widespread hope that the union might at last do something for jazz musicians. A lot of them had dropped their membership, and those who had stayed in were dissatisfied. The local held a large meeting, attended by two hundred or more, in its barn-like union hall in the old, art deco McGraw-Hill building on West 42nd Street, to which musicians were invited whether they were members or not. The musicians kicked the union around for all its sins of the previous sixty years, including racism and neglect of freelance artists.

After the meeting, the union's administration found a way to help them when drummer Bill Eldridge brought the officers a copy of the cabaret ordinance. Most jazz musicians had been harassed by it at one time or another, either because they played an instrument forbidden in unlicensed places, or because they could not play with the musicians they wanted. Pianists were barred from working in a trio with a drummer, an otherwise natural combination, and singers were barred from working with more than a guitar or a piano. The definition in the ordinance seemed to the musicians to be directed at just the instruments and combinations that were typical of jazz.

That same year, the union leadership helped to draft a bill for an amendment to the cabaret ordinance that turned out, for political reasons, to have a very limited scope. It did no more than eliminate the discrimination among instruments by redefining "incidental musical entertainment" to be music produced by mechanical devices or three live musicians playing any instruments. There was a question among the rank and file whether trying to eliminate the discrimination, and nothing more, was useful at all—whether a broader attack on the restriction of the *number* of instruments was not what was really needed. As a practical matter, the broader attack would eliminate the "incidental musical entertainment" category altogether, taking restaurants and bars with live music only—without social dancing or other entertainment—out of the definition of a cabaret. City officials advising the union were not ready to make that jump, and argued that working on the discrimination alone was at least worth a try. Some union members grudgingly agreed. The saxophonist Sonny Fortune told me years later that he thought *any* change would be helpful. Fortune felt it was important to get the restaurants thinking in terms of live music, "to create a situation where live music is expected," whether or not the restaurants had groups larger than a trio. Besides, he said, "the old law was ridiculous. You couldn't even have a flute under the old law."[4]

By 1985, Local 802 was campaigning very hard for the rights of horns and percussion under the bill. In March, which was, ironically, declared "cabaret month" by the City, the musicians held a press conference in front of City Hall. The press loved it, running a picture of Warren Chiasson, whose vibraphone was technically "percussion," playing in the snow. Editorial opinion seemed for the most part to buy the musicians' argument that canned music or other urban noises were much louder than live music; the *Daily News* ran a cartoon by Paul Rigby, now the frontispiece of this book, showing the police raiding a club in front of which a construction crew is tearing up the sidewalk with jackhammers, while one officer says to another, "Surround the place, I think I hear one of those rowdy jazzmen in there!"[5] It was shortly after this that I awoke to the problem and called Local 802.

Despite the press support, as Chapter Five will recount in detail, I became persuaded as the year wore on that the amended ordinance, even in its narrowly limited form, was not going to pass. Furthermore, the City's Department of Consumer Affairs seemed to have started a crackdown on unlicensed clubs. The union identified twenty-five clubs, most of them quite obscure, that were closed in the year ending in March 1986. Then the City summonsed some that were better known, like Preacher's on Bleecker Street, the West End Bar, on Broadway near 113th Street, and the Angry Squire, on Seventh Avenue near 23rd Street.[6] The reasons for the sudden spate of enforcement were unclear, although some musicians, such as Sonny Fortune and Warren Chiasson, suspected that it was a reaction to the union's effort to get the law changed. That was plausible, although I somehow doubted it; I did not think we were enough of a threat even to stir the bureaucratic leviathan to action. But at that time I could offer no other explanation.

The union officers were still not ready to join a lawsuit, because they thought that filing it would anger the City and the councilmembers, destroying any remaining chance for favorable action on the bill. I was not surprised that the union supposed that a lawsuit would merely drive the City to entrench its position. Such a reaction is supposed to be a classic drawback to Anglo-American litigation, and lawsuits, especially private suits and suits for damages, sometimes do have that effect. My experience of litigation against municipalities had been different, at least in cases where a law or a regulation was under attack as a matter of principle, and no official's integrity or pocketbook was under attack. In such cases, I had found, litigation often made it easier to get a law or a regulation changed; it was a way of shifting the agenda, of forcing attention to the problem, especially by the City's lawyers.[7] No doubt the difference between me and the union lay partly in the simple fact that I was a litigating lawyer; it is in the nature of the beast to have at least a grain of optimism about the outcome of cases. I did not know then what the union's experience with the law had been, how often court decisions and legislation had made their work more difficult. If I had known then the history told in the next chapter, I would have been even less surprised that the union was cautious.

I began to talk to musicians to see if a suit was a possibility. One was Warren Chiasson, the vibraphonist, who had been interested in the reform from the start. Chiasson later described his experiences with the system in his affidavit seeking an injunction in the lawsuit:

> I am originally from Nova Scotia . . . where I worked as a musician. From 1959–62, I toured with the George Shearing group, playing the vibraphone. Following that period, I settled in New York, which is a center for jazz and jazz musicians.
>
> The following year, I formed my own group, a trio with two other well-known musicians, Teddy Kotick on bass and Roland Hanna on piano. We had a job in 1963 at the Five Spot Cafe, a famous jazz club which was then located on St. Marks Place near the corner of Third Avenue in Manhattan. I believe that it did not have a cabaret license. My group and I played for about three nights at the club; after that the police came to the club and said that the vibraphone could not be used because it was a percussion instrument. Roland Hanna and Teddy

> Kotick went on and played for some time at the club, but I was not able to play because I played the vibraphone. Thus I was prevented from playing with a group that I myself had organized.

Chiasson went on to describe other places from which he had been excluded. Particularly striking was his experience at Gregory's:

> In 1974, I started to work at a bar and restaurant called Gregory's, located at 1149 First Avenue, Manhattan. I played vibraphone there for years, and drew a good business to the place, including music lovers from abroad. The manager of the place, Norman Silver, told me finally that he had been informed by the authorities that it was not legal to have a vibraphone playing in the place, and that he had to let me go. I now work there only Tuesday evenings as a pianist.[8]

I also talked to Mark Morganelli, later to be the second plaintiff in the case. He was a young trumpet and flugelhorn player, who had run a well-known place, the Jazz Forum, without a license, and was still organizing gigs at other clubs. In the lawsuit, he, too, described his experiences:

> During 1986, I have played at the Angry Squire, at 216 Seventh Avenue. I played there on February 28 and March 1, 1986. I am informed that at about that time the Angry Squire received a summons for violating the cabaret laws, and that I cannot be booked there while the present law concerning wind and percussion instruments is in effect.
>
> I have been asked by the management at the West End Cafe, 2911 Broadway in Manhattan, to organize and play at music sessions on Tuesday nights in April, May and June of this year [i.e. 1986]. I am informed that the West End Cafe, like the Angry Squire, has recently

received a summons for violating the cabaret laws and has paid a fine. I am thus prevented from organizing and playing in those sessions in the immediate future.[9]

As word began to get around that a case was in the works, people took me aside to give me advice. One old hand in the music world advised me not to work with the union, saying "they don't give a damn for jazz musicians." I had heard that one often enough not to argue with it; I just reminded him that the union had a fund of information and indispensable contacts with thousands of musicians. Besides, the whole attack on "incidental musical entertainment" was really the union's project. The man went on to urge me to press on beyond the mere discrimination in instruments to attack the three-musician limitation.

Shortly afterward, I had lunch with a soft-spoken lawyer, Peter Sims, known to the jazz world as the exceptional drummer, Pete LaRoca, a name he adopted working in latin bands, where his true last name was almost unpronounceable. Sims was also concerned that the case should not be limited to the discrimination against winds and percussion. Jazz is rarely played in trio form, he reminded me, and just eliminating the discrimination was not going to solve the problem for the musicians. We discussed the theory of the suit, which we both thought should be brought as a First Amendment case, based on the rights of free expression of the musicians. Sims didn't want me to forget that there is just as strong an interest in playing the music with a group large enough, and with the proper voicings, to express the leader's and side musicians' musical ideas, as there is in playing a particular instrument.

In the spring of 1986, the union officers finally reached such a point of frustration with the legislative process, of which more in Chapter Five, that they were ready for a lawsuit, including an attack on the three-musician rule. Our urgent problem, as I saw it, even before we could apply for some relief from a court, was to understand how the patchwork system of regulation had come into being. But my narrow litigator's view missed what was really going on behind even this basic question. Several actors, each with an idiosyncratic history, were being brought together to bring about, or to frustrate, a political change in the City. They were the musicians union, the clubs and the musicians who played in them, and the municipal regulatory system of which the cabaret licenses were a part.

CHAPTER 2

THE MUSICIANS UNION

In 1983, at the time of the membership meeting with the jazz musicians and the decision to try to change the "incidental music exception" in the cabaret laws, the newly elected officers of Local 802 of the American Federation of Musicians were confronted with a host of problems that earlier leaders had failed to solve or had even perpetuated.

From before the turn of the century, musicians had some of the most close-knit local organizations in the American labor movement. The New York musicians formed a close shop that withstood legal challenge as early as 1890;[1] the closed shop later became part of a fixed rule throughout the national union, the American Federation of Musicians (AFM), forbidding members to play with anyone who was not a member. We might think of this as part of a set of guild traditions requiring members to adhere to their rules, and to stick together against outsiders. Local 802 still has a bylaw, never formally enforced, forbidding members "to commit any act tending to injure the reputation of a fellow member in his/her calling as a musician."[2]

Although music has always been an elaborate craft, with "mysteries" closed to outsiders, tight discipline was necessary if the organization was to be effective, because the centrifugal forces against it were and still are enormous. Throughout its existence, the union has been disrupted by "technological" un-employment. The advent of talking pictures, for example, threw thousands of members who accompanied the silents out of work.[3] James C. Petrillo, having witnessed that shrinkage of jobs, was determined to resist the next great decimation after he became president of the AFM in 1940. The use of musical recordings for broadcasts threatened to eliminate hundreds of jobs in radio, without any compensation to the musicians; a strike by musicians against the broadcasters was not very likely to be effective when the broadcasters could simply replace the musicians with recordings. To forestall the broadcasters, Petrillo called his most notorious job-action, a boycott of all recording sessions by union members, that ran for many months in 1942 and 1943. The ban made Petrillo's name synonymous in the press with "dictatorial" and "featherbedding" labor tactics. Hardly daunted, Petrillo called a similar ban in 1948. Both of these resulted in payments into trust funds established for musicians.[4]

More importantly, the bans resulted in a national outcry against Petrillo, and in legislation directed against organized labor in general and the musicians union in particular. A direct result was the Lea Act of 1946, which introduced penalties for threats and other tactics to induce broadcasters to use musicians they did not want. In the Taft-Hartley Act of the next year, the featherbedding provisions as well as perhaps the secondary boycott restrictions were influenced by experiences with the musicians union.[5]

Petrillo's world is difficult to imagine at this distance in time. He came out of an environment in which all music was played live, in which one did not hear music except when produced by an individual or an orchestra. He was never really interested in player pianos, recordings, moving picture soundtracks, broadcasting or any other form of mechanical reproduction. He was interested in work for live musicians, and in particular he organized the thousands who had been thrown out of work. Thus Petrillo never invested much effort in getting royalties for the musicians who made recordings, who were only a small fraction of the union, but instead saw to it that the trust funds were used to employ other musicians in concerts.

Petrillo also had little faith in government aid to labor, either through legislation or the courts; having come into the labor movement long before the New Deal, he saw direct action as the quickest and most effective tactic for organized labor.[6] One result was that a large part of the public, including a great many musicians, came to dislike him intensely. His tactics provoked legislative action such as the Lea Act that only made the musicians more isolated than they had been before. The union has since come to accept that a public-be-damned attitude is the wrong approach for an entertainment union. Although union officials try to make use of government, through lobbying and the courts, they are cautious because their experience has not been encouraging.

In the forties, when Petrillo took his notorious job actions, according to Vern Countryman, "the AFM had practically every professional instrumental performer and conductor in the United States enrolled as a member." There were 28,000 members in New York's Local 802 alone.[7] And despite the incursions of technology that Petrillo was vainly trying to hold back, cultural expectations about live music were much more encouraging for musicians than they are now. When people went out to an elegant place to dance, or even just to dine, they expected to hear a live orchestra. Even less elegant places, such as strip joints and taxi-dance halls, where patrons hired the women who worked in the hall to dance with them, had live music. Charlie Parker had his first music job in New York at a taxi-dance hall, and as late as the 1950s I went to hear some forgotten older jazz musicians who were making a living by playing in one of the last of these halls, the New Gardens on Fourteenth Street.[8] While union contracts undoubtedly helped to maintain those jobs, so did public expectations. Live music was identified with dancing and a good time; one expected to dance or see dancing performed with a band.

Its organization was so strong that the union made little use of the procedures under the federal labor laws for certifying its affiliates through election as the collective bargaining agents at the various places where their members played.[9] The AFM maintained its power through internal discipline extended to employers through the union's virtual monopoly of the supply of music. Thus it was difficult for a musician to work outside the union or for any establishment to hire a band unless it was a union band. A friend of mine who is an amateur reed player tells of playing at a dance on Long Island with some other teenage friends as late as the early sixties; the union representative came by, flanked by two silent companions in dark suits, and told them that they would join the union that week if they wanted to keep playing.

The union would, through contract, set a minimum pay scale for a place, depending on its size and type. Thus a small jazz club could have a lower scale than a popular dance spot. Leaders as well as side musicians were union members; representatives would come around to make sure that only union people were at work, and that there were no more people on the stand than the contract called for. The leader had to discipline the band in accordance with union rules, on pain of being tried and fined by the union.

This apparent solidarity concealed status and class conflicts and jealousies. Concert instrumentalists, conductors and singers resisted affiliation, apparently thinking it beneath them, until the AFM forced it upon them by refusing to allow members to perform with them as accompanists or in any other way.[10] Thus various categories of classical musicians showed that they felt themselves superior to other classical musicians, not to speak of those who played popular music. Less fortunate musicians felt, and still feel, resentment against symphony musicians, who are thought to bargain for and receive special privileges. Jazz musicians think of themselves, quite justifiably in most cases, as "scuffling" and "paying dues," and they resent the "squares" who don't have to do the same thing. Classical musicians, in turn, for years disdained the jazz world as crime-infested and the musicians as poorly trained. In addition, there are "studio" musicians who play mostly uncredited music for broadcast, recording and film, as well as "club date" musicians who play in orchestras for single engagements at prom dances, weddings and the like (The term "club date" never refers to a date played in a jazz club, but rather to single engagements in places such as country clubs). Although a musician may make his or her way from one group to another, each of them has special problems or advantages that set one group apart from the others. It is little wonder that Local 802 saw the need for a rule prohibiting its members from disparaging one another's work.

During the forty-odd years since the Taft-Hartley Act, the iron system of organization among American musicians has gradually rusted and weakened. Expectations about live music have changed apace, to the point where a great many listeners would rather hear a recording, with all its special electronic enhancement, than live music, and many popular bands actually cannot produce in person the effects achieved in their recordings. The Milli Vanilli scandal of 1990, in which it was revealed that the stars did not sing on their own prize-winning popular recording, was but the end of a long process. And a "discotheque" is, after all, by definition a place where the patrons dance to recordings.

Technological change is exploding. In 1984, Warner Communications installed a robot pop singer called Sammy Sands, complete with gestures, in a cafe in Georgia, hoping to use it as a showcase to sell the robot nationally. While Sammy Sands does not seem so far to have caught the fancy of the public, much more dismaying problems loom. Some New York theatrical producers have been threatening to use a synthesizer in place of the orchestra for musical shows, a potential catastrophe for New York musicians comparable to the elimination of live music from the motion picture theaters. So far the union has successfully resisted the threat.[11]

Equally important, the guild rules by which the union traditionally protected the mysteries of music have run up against problems in the labor laws that make it increasingly difficult to maintain discipline in the face of unemployment. A true closed shop, in which the musician is required to be a member of the local before he can work, was made legally unenforceable under the Taft-Hartley Act. The Act set a thirty-day period during which an employee can work at a job before joining the union.[12] However much this might make sense in the world of the industrial job for a single employer, in which the employee may want to work for a month to find out whether he likes the job and the union before he pays his dues, it is largely unworkable in the world of one-night stands and short engagements that is usually the lot of the popular musician. In the club date field, the dance band usually works for the employer only once, and in a jazz club, a week's engagement is a long one. It seems that an unwilling musician could not be recruited into the union under those conditions, because he would virtually never work at a job for thirty days.[13]

Local 802 has been able to maintain union wages and fringe benefits in some situations, for example in many club date orchestras in New York, like those of Peter Duchin or Lester Lanin. Even though the musicians in the club date bands may play for each employer only once, they usually play for a single band or a group of bands over a long period of time. So long as the club date musicians are willing to stick together and bargain, and the bandleaders are able to pass the costs (sometimes with a nice profit) on to the colleges, caterers and fathers-of-the-bride, standards can be maintained.[14]

For musicians who play at jazz clubs in New York City the benefits of union organization are more vague. Under the old system of internal control, the union would set a pay scale for a club, frequently very low, but would not effectively extract pension or health benefits; under present conditions, as I will shortly explain in more detail, it often cannot even do that much. The "bandleader" of a jazz band usually does not have the same power, either in relation to his musicians or the employer, that the club date bandleader has; he is simply the person who makes the deal for the gig and gets the band together. He is a musician like the others, not someone with whom other players could or would want to bargain very effectively. And if they do try to bargain with him for better pay, the club's leverage is usually overwhelming. There are so many more musicians than there are jobs, that the club owner can get another band that will work for whatever he wants to offer; then the first band does not get its chance to be heard, which often is the only point in getting the job in the first place. It is not like the club date field, in which the next band is going to ask for the same rates, or perhaps refuse to play at all.

The possibility of a job action, such as a strike and a picket line, is limited by the ease with which musicians can be replaced, as a consequence not only of unemployment, but also of a generalized change in attitudes in the United States. An increasing number of workers throughout the economy today are not unionized; the percentage of those in unions is less than half what it was in the fifties.[15] With the decrease in union solidarity, it has become socially acceptable for a person who needs a job to replace one who is on strike. Since the late thirties, it has been legally permissible for an employer to hire permanent replacements for strikers,[16] but employers hesitated to do it until the eighties, fearing retaliation and permanently embittered labor relations. The public perception was changed by the federal air traffic controllers strike of 1981, when President Reagan succeeded in systematically replacing strikers by the thousands. Since that time, both employers and other workers have become much more willing to replace strikers.[17] In the atmosphere that has prevailed in the eighties, with plenty of good musicians around, some of them disaffected from the union, a group of players or their union local are not going to undertake a job action unless they are pretty sure that potential replacements are sympathetic. And correspondingly, adherence to the union is weakened.

Even under the best of conditions, when musicians are most favorable to organization by the union, the capacity of the union to bargain collectively for them under the terms of the Taft-Hartley Act is sometimes not clear. Since the inception of the

National Labor Relations Act in the thirties, only those who can properly be called "employees" have been permitted to combine to bargain about working conditions. Significantly, we think of an employee as one who works "under" or whose work is "controlled by" another. The governing idea is that the Labor Act was not supposed to aid those, loosely categorized as "independent contractors," who are themselves entrepreneurs, especially those who employ others. Thus sub-contractors and the like, even though they produce work that is part of a larger job, are not viewed as "employees" of those for whom they do the work, because the law holds that they do not need the support of the labor laws to enable them to combine to maintain their wages and other benefits. In theory, the law makes a radical distinction, forbidding combinations of entrepreneurs to protect their profits while it encourages combinations of workers to protect their wages.[18]

That legal distinction cuts across more complex economic relations in modern life brought about by the division of labor. In fact, virtually all producers are interdependent; nearly every working individual, however strong, is dependent on others and could use some protection against the pressures of those more powerful. Nevertheless the National Labor Relations Act sought to separate only those who were particularly susceptible to exploitation for protection as "employees" under the labor laws.

Before 1947, the Supreme Court adopted a flexible test, trying as a practical matter to single out those who were really wage earners, subject to dismissal or other punishment if they tried to bargain alone. In a case upholding the right of newsboys to organize and bargain collectively with their newspaper, as against the claim that they were independent contractors, the Court said, "the mischief at which the Act is aimed and the remedies it offers are not confined exclusively to employees within the traditional legal distinctions separating them from 'independent contractors'," and went on, "it cannot be irrelevant that the particular workers in these cases are subject, as a matter of economic fact, to the evils the statute was designed to eradicate and that the remedies it affords are appropriate for preventing them or curing their harmful effects in the special situation."[19] While this formulation was subject to the objection that it was vague, the Court was at least trying to come to grips with the social purposes that underlay the Labor Act.

The drafters of the 1947 Taft-Hartley amendments attacked this functional distinction between employees and independent contractors, claiming that Congress had all along meant the term "employee" to be used only as it had been before the Labor Act was passed. When Congress amended the definition of employee specifically to exclude "independent contractors," Senator Taft explained:

> The legal effect of the amendment . . . is merely to make it clear that the question whether or not a person is an employee is always a question of law, since the term is not meant to embrace persons outside that category under the general principles of the law of agency.[20]

The "general principles of the law of agency" for separating independent contractors from employees include a set of seemingly neutral, humdrum factors. Among them are the extent of control exercised by the employer over the details of the work, whether the work is customarily done with or without supervision, the skill required, whether the employer supplies the tools and the place of work, the duration of the employment, whether payment is by time or by the job, and whether or not the work is part of the regular business of the employer.[21] These might work well in deciding, for example, whether an employer ought to have to pay for the wrongs of his "servant," to use the traditional term. They create confusion, however, when they are applied to the decision whether workers are covered by the Labor Act.

Senator Taft's position was a classic example of the use of formalistic legal arguments for hidden policy purposes. Congress was able to turn the matter into what appeared to be a dry "lawyer's dispute," ignoring the question of whether the older

distinctions could be used to determine who really had the economic need for the power of collective bargaining under the
Labor Act. What concerned Congress under the surface, however, was that the Supreme Court's ruling in the newsboys' case
had been used to expand the universe of protected workers.
As Marc Linder has remarked, ". . .the amended definition of
'employee' was part and parcel of the general intention of Taft-
Hartley to confine the scope and power of unions."[22]

The courts have struggled to apply the definition of "independent contractor" in the formalistic way that Taft wanted. More
than thirty years after the Taft-Hartley Act, the District of Columbia Circuit was still able to write:

> It is very significant . . . as the Senator noted, that the
> 'question whether or not a person is an employee is
> always a question of law.' . . . .It is a legal conclusion
> to be drawn from the facts—not a question of policy.[23]

This is not really possible, of course; a legal conclusion of this
sort cannot be drawn except in the light of policy. Not surprisingly, the results have been inconsistent from the point of view
of labor-law policy; the results sometimes succeed and sometimes fail in protecting those who need to have the power to
bargain collectively.

The formalistic approach has caused problems for groups of
workers through the economy, from farm workers to cabdriv-
ers, as employers have tried to escape from collective bargaining
or to avoid paying employee benefits. The problems are particularly intractable in the case of musicians, both because they are
artists who often express themselves in a highly individual way,
and because they frequently work through a leader in dealing
with their employer and the public.

It is easy to see how a wooden application of the traditional
factors for the employee/independent contractor distinction
could lead to the conclusion that almost any musician, but especially a jazz musician working in a club, is an independent
contractor. The musician brings her own tools (unless she plays

an acoustic piano), displays great skill, is paid by the job— usually one of short duration—and is typically a luxury rather than a necessity in the business of selling food or liquor. And if she is a jazz musician, she does not want or get much direction from the club owner about what she plays. She plays something at least a little different every night and the better she is, the more discretion she has in playing it. From the point of view of her playing, the jazz musician is practically the musical embodi- ment of an independent contractor; independence is one of her defining characteristics.

For the musician's relation to the club owner, however, this musical independence does not make much difference. She is going to get the same pay regardless what she plays, and be replaced by some equally independent artist if she squawks too much about it.

Here is a case where the formalistic test is misleading, unless the factors are interpreted in a sophisticated way. The employer supplies the place of work, and usually controls the work in a general way. He chooses the musicians for their style of music, and expects them to play within it. He dictates the times the musicians will show up, and when the music will be played. Although he pays by the job, he often pays the same amount each night, even to varying groups of musicians. And so forth. The point here is not to parse these legal arguments; the point instead is that, although the traditional tests can be harnessed to the economic relations between musicians and their employers, this formal approach tends to blur the central inquiry of whether the relationship between the employer and the musicians is such that the musicians need a collective bargaining agent. It is usually possible for an employer to make at least a plausible argument that a jazz musician is an independent contractor.

The situation is complicated by the fact that musical groups almost always have a leader. Some leaders truly are independent, in the sense that they run the band, write or buy its arrangements, and have a "name" that gives them plenty of leverage in dealing with employers. They lead the band over a long period, bargain with the employer, usually for a single appearance, and pay the musicians, who are often anonymous as far as the employer is concerned.

But a band has a leader, ultimately, because it is in the nature of music played collectively that it requires someone to choose the instrumentation and give the music direction. At the typical jazz gig, the leader does bargain with the club owner, and brings the musicians together. He will choose the numbers to be played, roughly lay out each piece by indicating who is to take solos, and sometimes write arrangements, although other members of the band may do the same. He may even get paid a little more than the side musicians. But the leader status is just as much for the employer's convenience, so that he has only one person to negotiate with and pay. And the bandleader's bargaining power is typically no greater than that of any other member of the band; one of the side musicians may organize the band for the next engagement. Nevertheless, it is easy for a club owner to argue that the leaders of such bands are independent contractors. They have all the artistic independence of jazz musicians, together with some of the indicia of real leadership independence, even though they may be completely at the mercy of club owners because their band can be immediately replaced by another.

The musicians union has had a lot of difficulty with the argument that its members who play freelance jobs at jazz clubs are not "employees" of the club, entitled to have the union bargain for them. The courts have never ruled authoritatively that single musicians, such as pianists who play in a bar, can be viewed as independent contractors with whom the union cannot form a collective bargaining relation. But it is always at least a respectable claim, that has to be argued out anew in the case of every club.

The situation with bands has been even more chancy; the courts have sometimes held against the union, finding that bandleaders are independent contractors. In the case of the Puerto Rican Hotel Association, for example, the Second Circuit Court of Appeals in New York City held in 1982 that the musicians in the house orchestras were not employees of the hotels, even though their relation was a long-standing one, chiefly because the bandleaders selected the repertoire and the musicians, and because the hotels dealt with the bands through the leaders.[24] The effect of such a decision is that the musicians, represented by the union, have to bargain with the bandleader for wages and pension and other benefits, and that the ultimate purchaser, the hotel, can refuse to bargain with the union. It is possible to maintain standards if the band members are unified, and if the leader has some bargaining power with the hotel, even though the bargaining strength of the union is lost. But in the case of a typical jazz group, in a short engagement using a rather nominal leader, the members cannot effectively bargain with the leader, nor the leader with the club.

In addition to all these problems, according to the present leadership, the local wasted what sources of strength and credibility it still had with its members before 1983. The local had formed cozy relations with some employers, so that members could not increase their benefits or express an effective grievance.[25] The local had notoriously bad relations with jazz musicians; as I heard one union officer mutter, "the union never did anything for the jazz musician but put its hand in his pocket." The union failed for the most part to organize the clubs, and when scale was set by the union, it was still very low. Pension and welfare benefits were frequently not collected from clubs. Yet the business agents still came around to make sure that everyone on the bandstand was a member and that only the prescribed number of musicians were playing—a particularly exasperating requirement for jazz musicians, who like to sit in with other bands. In the status hierarchy of the union, the jazz musicians felt like poor relations. Little wonder that all the problems of learning to play and getting accepted in the business were lumped under the expression "paying dues." The union repeated the mistake later on with rock musicians, failing for the most part to organize them or recruit them into the union.

There was also widespread discrimination against black musicians, which the union did little to dispel. Milt Hinton, the grandfather of modern jazz bassists, says that he once got a job playing in a big club date band, which for him was almost unprecedented. When he got to the date, he found that it was an NAACP convention, for which he was the token black player. On another occasion, many years ago, he complained to a union official that some black players were being paid for recordings in cash and off the books, under circumstances where they would not receive pension and other benefits. The official suggested that Hinton should not complain because, as he said, "these are your boys." Hinton inferred some cozy relation between the union official and the record company.[26]

In the face of all these problems—technological unemployment combined with corresponding changes in public taste, lack of a formal collective bargaining relation with many employers, the end of the closed shop and the generalized decline of a sense of union solidarity, the growing argument that musicians are too independent to be "employees" for purposes of collective bargaining, and the sense of alienation of many potential members—the union has been declining in strength. At the time the case was brought against the cabaret-licensing system in 1986, Local 802 had fifteen thousand members,[27] a little over half what it had in 1948.

Fortunately, the local has been able to continue bargaining successfully and even to make improvements in situations where the musicians have a long-term relationship with one employer, or where the union has an established collective bargaining relation. The result is that many jazz musicians, particularly those who are a little older, seek those jobs and avoid the clubs. To take just one example, John Carisi, one of the first modern-jazz trumpeters and still a marvelous horn player, works consistently in the club date bands in New York. Carisi says, "The jazz clubs are all right if you are a loner. But if you have a family, and you want to own things like automobiles, they are no good."

Lawyer-drummer Peter LaRoca Sims put it in a different perspective: "The union is great for studio work, for symphony work, for club dates, or for Broadway. In those cases, you can have a job action if you have to. But it has been almost useless for free lancers."[28]

By 1983, the question was what the incoming administration at Local 802 could do to repair the situation. One of the things the union most dramatically needed, both at the local and national level, was some favorable change in the laws. It pursued the sort of political program at the city and state level that would have been anathema in the days of Petrillo. It lobbied successfully, for example, for a state law that shortened the waiting time to join the union to seven days for musicians, and it joined the national office in agitating for the passage of a set of Performing Arts Labor Relations Amendments that were aimed at eliminating the "independent contractor" objection to collective bargaining representation by the union.[29]

The local hired new organizers to replace the old business agents. One of them, David Sheldon, talked about the problems of organizing jazz musicians and clubs under the present legal restrictions.[30] There were so many musicians, many of them non-union, in relation to the jobs, he said, that expectations for pay had sunk very low. When Sheldon asked a group of players to name the minimum for which they would play a gig, they named figures between sixty and a hundred dollars, less than most New York lawyers get for an hour's work. And they were being brave; if they are short of work, many will play for less.

The union didn't want to go back to the old system of internal discipline, even if they could have done so under the Taft-Hartley Act. Using members to discipline others, Sheldon said, is too much like "punishing the victims." And under present circumstances, if the local tried to discipline a member, even a bandleader, for working with non-union people or accepting a job at minimal pay, the member would be very likely to resign from the union.[31]

Organizing the clubs, furthermore, is a daunting prospect. Every club, however small, has to be organized separately, with the potential for a representation fight in each case. A club may have literally dozens of players working over the course of a year, most of whom have to come to an agreement before a job action can effectively be taken or the local can officially be named as bargaining agent. And even when the musicians do take common action, the club can fight the issue by claiming that the musicians are independent contractors. The club called Greene Street Cafe in Soho has resisted the union with this argument, as did the Ravelled Sleave, a club on the Upper East Side, before the Labor Board ruled that the piano players there were indeed employees. These administrative proceedings, even when they are successful, are so protracted that they are not very useful to the individual musicians involved.[32] And if the union calls a strike against a club, there is little to prevent the place from hiring replacements. Sheldon says that pay and conditions are just as bad or worse in clubs that offer rock music, because there are even more bands that want to get a hearing in relation to the number of places that will hire them.

Nevertheless, clubs sometimes do get organized. Some places can be organized because they earn such a reputation for mistreating musicians that, after a time, no one they want to hire will work there. In 1987, a large number of musicians who played at a bar in Chelsea called Rick's Lounge picketed the place until it accepted an agreement.[33] Well-run places like Sweet Basil and the Village Vanguard, both on Seventh Avenue, a few blocks apart, have signed performance agreements because they like to have good relations with their musicians and the union. They recognise, as do the musicians, that labor disputes are an unnecessary diversion. The musicians want to play and be heard; that, after all, is the reason musicians go to play in places, not so well-known, that pay them almost nothing.

What the musicians wanted in 1983 was not coercion, either against themselves or the clubs: they wanted more jobs, more places to play. The union officers heard that clearly when they called their meeting to sound out the jazz musicians. An attack on restrictions in the cabaret laws was in many ways the perfect local issue. The union could work at the problem through its lobbying program, and, if the effort was successful, the change would create more work.

CHAPTER 3

THE MUSIC IN THE CLUBS

The legend about the migration of jazz in New York City is that it was first played Uptown in the twenties, when white people flocked to Harlem night clubs, then in Midtown in a crowded warren of clubs on West 52nd Street during the thirties and forties, and finally Downtown in Greenwich Village and neighborhoods south and east of the Village. As Arnold Shaw put it in his study of 52nd Street, "[v]iewed sociologically, 52d Street is the story of how Harlem came downtown—not only its music and dances, but its chicken and rib joints and its talented people."[1]

The legend is both true and an oversimplification. Since the twenties, jazz has been played all over town. Although it had appeared in New York earlier, jazz first became popular in 1917 when the Original Dixieland Jass Band played at Reisenweber's, a genuine cabaret, located at Columbus Circle at 59th Street. The music was considered a naughty novelty—the word "jass" referred to sexual intercourse—and with their white patrons the Harlem clubs were to trade on the suggestive innuendo through their dancing and floor shows as well as hot music. Lena Horne recalled, "[t]he shows had a primitive, naked quality that was supposed to make a civilized audience lose its inhibitions. The music had an intensive, pervasive rhythm—sometimes loud and brassy, often weird and wild. The dances were eloquently provocative . . . ." Many white people went Uptown with a shiver of adventure, supposedly to abandon the restraints of respectability; the effect was intensified by the fact that most Harlem clubs were among the few places in a segregated society where blacks and whites could mix. Although a few clubs catered almost exclusively to whites, more of them had mixed patronage; all the musicians who played in them regularly were black. Duke Ellington's band, when they finished playing to the white audience at the Cotton Club, went on to jam before a mixed audience at the Lenox Club down the street. The row of clubs along 133rd Street between Seventh and Lenox Avenues was called "Jungle Alley."[2]

But only, I suspect, by downtowners. Serious work was being done on the music in those clubs. Stride pianists had contests with Willie "the Lion" Smith in Pod's and Jerry's, and musicians jammed together after hours at places like Mexico's and the Nest. White musicians like Eddie Condon and Mezz Mezzrow came to play and learn. Condon, in fact, acted as a sort of broker to the commercial world Downtown, bringing musicians who played in Small's Paradise, the enormous club at 135th and Seventh, as well as Fats Waller from Connie's Inn, to RCA Victor for recordings.[3]

Harlem was showing the perennial elements of a strong jazz environment. The clubs not only supported the musicians, but gave them places to hone their skills and learn from one another. The complexity of learning to improvise, to make use of new rhythmic patterns and at the same time play with others, made for a difficult art that, to a large extent, had to be shaped in a group. Hours of playing together made good musicians able to react to nuances of style from others. They communicated excitement to one another, and to an audience, who then communicated a little of it back to them. The relation between the audience and the orchestras at the huge Savoy Ballroom in Harlem was legendary. Performance could create a tremendous sense of common emotional understanding and release. It was not surprising if white listeners, or black listeners who were not familiar with the rhythms or the exchange of ideas in an improvised art, experienced this as "abandonment." It turned out to be a historic misfortune that the forces of respectability identified the music with sexual abandon in a crude sense and that the purveyors capitalized on it; they played into the hands of early critics who condemned jazz as cacophonous on the one hand and insidiously immoral on the other.[4]

Because most of the Harlem clubs were illegal during the twenties, some of them felt a strong influence from bootleggers and other gangsters. The clubs on 52nd Street were speakeasies that emerged into the light after repeal, and sometimes also had underworld money invested in them. The Street, as 52nd Street was called, was a generalized entertainment district with no particular emphasis on music; in fact, of the thirty-odd places west of Fifth Avenue, only a handful ever catered to jazz. Some of the places were quite swell, like Jack and Charlie's "21," which is still on 52nd Street. The jazz clubs were mostly just "joints" in the sense we now understand the term—small and often shabby. They changed ownership and location quite often. A noted name like the Famous Door was at various times attached to four different clubs. As Jazz historian Leonard Feather described them, "all the clubs were shaped like shoe boxes, and they had dingy canopies outside. . . . Inside, there did not seem to be any difference, although I am sure that the colors of the walls, if you could see them through the cigarette smoke, were different. The tables were three inches square and the chairs were hard wood. The drinks were probably watered. They were miserable places. There was nothing to them but the music."[5] It was here, I think, that the jazz aficionado was born. These were places where one sat, practically face to face with a small band, and drank in the music. And to those who went to listen to the music, the cabaret-style nightclubs like Leon & Eddie's, or clubs like "21," were foreign territory.

The jazz clubs were originally musicians' hangouts. One of the earliest of them, the Onyx, did not even employ a band at first; the musicians came to play for themselves. As the Street developed, musicians would go from place to place and sit in with other bands, often causing a conflict with the union representatives, who objected to seeing a musician on the stand when he was not listed in the contract.[6] There were enough clubs, close enough together, that musicians could get to know one another and one another's work intimately. Some musicians, like Art Tatum, did their best work after hours and only really flourished when most of the public had gone to bed.

As elements of jazz were diluted into a commercial product in dance bands and broadcast work, musicians came to the clubs on the Street after hours to relax and play as they wished. The Chicago-style saxophonist Bud Freeman fled Ray Noble's band to play there, as pianist Johnny Guarnieri later escaped from Raymond Scott.[7] Some of the informal, personal expression of the music was slightly formalized and presented to the public in jam sessions at the Hickory House and Jimmy Ryan's; the audience crowded in to share the euphoria and excitement.

As certain clubs became popular, the music they featured sometimes grew more commercial, and serious musicians moved on to other places. The Famous Door was first funded by studio musicians disgusted with the increasing popularization of the Onyx and looking for a place to play and listen. Musicians came there with relief; the clowning of the band at the Onyx, where the song "The Music Goes 'Round and 'Round" had been popularized, drove Eddie Condon to go to work at the Famous Door with Bunny Berigan on trumpet.[8] One of the managers of the Onyx later told Arnold Shaw:

> Musicians made 52nd. They brought the radio crowd, the music publishers, the talent-agency execs, the theater people, the advertising guys—and finally the college kids, the society set, the cloak-and-suiters and the public. Name musicians made The Street into glamorville, with the help of the columnists. But as the public rushed in, the musicians walked out. And when the musicians took a powder, the public wasn't there. It's funny. By themselves, the musicians couldn't provide the business to

keep any clubs in business. But they wanted out, as the public came in to provide the finances.[9]

There were a good many jobs on the Street, because most of the clubs hired two bands, one with a bit of a name, and a relief band that was often just as interesting. But a pattern was developing that has continued intermittently up to the present. Although they were small, the clubs paid high rents, they were often on the edge financially, and the musicians suffered the consequences. As late as the 1940s, side musicians were still being paid seventy-five dollars a week, then a living wage, but not munificent. The pay in the Harlem clubs was even poorer.[10]

The musicians developed the love-hate relationship they still have with jazz clubs. They value them for what is to be learned from others and the enthusiasm created by the interplay with musicians and the audience. They hate them because some of those who run them can be exploitative and dishonest. The audience as well as the owners are often unappreciative of the best musicians, while they make celebrities out of some who are relatively mediocre. Some jazz musicians have rejected the club life altogether as unworthy of a serious artist,[11] pointing out that European music does not get played for a pittance in front of an audience made up in part of uncomprehending drunks. But the club life seems to be necessary to the life of jazz, at least for younger musicians; they use it to develop the indispensable sense of improvisatory participation in front of an audience.

The hours in the clubs were long, running from around nine-thirty to three in the morning or later, and the demands on creativity were even greater when the musicians went on to play for one another after hours. The sense of camaraderie was strong, and many players drank and some took drugs as part of the excitement. The bond created by inventing the music together, within an environment of a popular audience, was to make the musicians as a group both exclusive—contemptuous of the square world—and at the same time down to earth, democratic, unpretentious. It is notable how many jazz musicians do not use a real first name, but a nickname—"Dizzy," or "Sonny,"—or a diminutive—"Jackie" or "Eddie." Some have rejected this custom—Charles Mingus systematically tried to refuse to answer to the diminutive "Charlie"—but it goes on to this day. Musicians did put on airs; Willie "the Lion" Smith used to brag about his triumphs as a pianist, referring to himself in the story as "the Lion."[12] The idea seems to be that after having "scuffled" to play the music under such circumstances one might be elegant, like Duke Ellington, or unstable and unpredictable, like Bud Powell, but one might not be stuffy. It was a way of life that excited both admiration and contempt from outsiders.

Some who came into jazz were unstable and miserable apart from their work. The music gave their lives structure and meaning, but the musicians' life could not give them much help apart from the music. The audience was to make a few of them into sacred monsters, objects of reverence and terror. Their admirers believed, and others feared, that their wisdom in the music came from their rejection of and inability to accept ordinary standards.

Musicians came from Harlem to play on 52nd Street; Willie the Lion worked in the Onyx just as he had on 133rd Street. Very few black customers came to the Street, however, and the Harlem places did not disappear; after hours on 52nd Street, musicians often still went Uptown. White customers continued to come to the Harlem clubs, although they were less fashionable, particularly after the race-riot of 1935[13] rent the mask of good relations between blacks and whites.

Two Harlem clubs, Minton's on 118th Street and Monroe's at 133rd and Seventh Avenue, catered to musicians. Minton's was designed for musicians, and Monroe's was an ordinary night club with an after-hours policy.[14] It was here, and in other lesser-known places, that swing musicians gradually expanded the harmonic and rhythmic resources of the music into bebop. It was an aggressive, esoteric music, difficult to understand or to play, and deliberately so. It was meant to be revolutionary, the way jazz had been when it first sprang upon the music world in the early twenties.

Such a music developed its share of sacred monsters, including Charlie Parker and Bud Powell, as well as a set of hip attitudes. Of the saxophonist Jackie McLean, A.B. Spellman wrote, "It was in this era that the idea of hip developed, and Jackie is one of the last of the original hip musicians. They created a language, a dress, a music and a high which were closed unto themselves and allowed them to one-up the rest of the world. The bebop era was the first time that the black ego was expressed in America with self-assurance, and heroin, because its effect blocks out all doubt, is a drug that facilitates the self-assurance."[15] Bop was so exclusively an art of black musicians at that time, that it was news when a white musician could pick it up. Dizzy Gillespie said, "You remember Johnny Carisi? He was the only white boy up at Minton's. He'd learn all the tunes. Played all of Thelonious Monk's tunes, all of mine. I'd play a chorus. He'd be right behind me. . . . He was welcome so long as he could blow the way he did."[16] Jazz musicians were perhaps more in conflict with the respectable world, including a lot of union members and other musicians who did not like jazz, than they had been at any time since the twenties. During the Second World War, syndicated columnist Westbrook Pegler branded jazz "low" and "dirty" and bebop was called "degenerate."[17]

Gillespie, Parker and the others took the music Downtown to the Street during the forties, because that was the way to obtain access to a larger music world, and perhaps also because the pay was slightly better than in Harlem. They worked with bassist Oscar Pettiford, guitarist Tiny Grimes and with swing musicians who had not yet assimilated the new ideas. By this time, Harlem had begun to invest in the Street; Clark Monroe, owner of the Uptown club, Monroe's, opened the Spotlite.

In the late forties, as many commentators have remarked, a visitor could get a history of jazz by walking down 52nd Street.[18] There were traditional musicians from New Orleans and Chicago, contemporary swing musicians from all over, and the bop musicians from Harlem. Almost everyone who had ever played jazz was still working. Although some of the great pioneers were dead, an astounding number were alive; there were major, original creators from every style who worked on the Street and elsewhere in town.

Yet the revolution that was bop was causing a counter-revolution, fragmenting the music into schools. There was a revival of interest in the traditional jazz from New Orleans and Chicago; ideologues rejected most of the music that was characteristic of New York, including the small-band swing of the thirties and forties. Thinking only of the traditional jazz players, the editor of Eddie Condon's memoirs rashly wrote in 1947, "there are no more than half a hundred first class players of jazz."[19] A group of young men from Scarsdale led by Bob Wilber was reviving the music of King Oliver's Creole Band, and finding it dauntingly difficult to play; their trumpeter, John Glasel, emerged as the president of Local 802 thirty-odd years later after playing jazz and every other sort of music. The hipsters who supported bop were equally exclusive, shunning everything first played before 1940. Small-band swing began to pass completely under a cloud.

In retrospect, this was a great misfortune. Although I admit, to my shame, that as a teenager in the fifties I was one of the "moldy fig" traditionalists, I think all of us sectarians were wasting irretrievable resources. When I went to hear the band at the New Gardens taxi-dance hall on 14th Street, I heard musicians of all the older New York eras. From the swing bands there were Rudy Powell on sax and Abe Bolar on bass. The most interesting figure was Ed Allen, once star of the Clarence Williams band, one of the first jazz bands in New York. He was still quite able, and it was illuminating to hear a player who derived his inspiration from the days before Louis Armstrong shaped all the trumpeters.[20] But it was not a jazz band. When the musicians found out that visitors were interested in what they could really do, they dusted off—literally—an arrangement of "Honeysuckle Rose." After the first chorus, the dirty old men who frequented the place looked like they were going to suffer seizures and the manager immediately bustled in to put a stop to the excitement.

In the fifties, music declined on 52nd Street, primarily for economic reasons; the club owners who cared about music had little by little sold out to those who wanted to make money any way they could, chiefly through striptease (often still accompanied by jazz, in strange accordance with older attitudes toward the music). The Hickory House was one of the few places that continued a vigorous jazz policy.

Promoters found that young people were willing to pay an admission charge to sit respectfully and listen to jazz in large halls, where they cared very little about buying booze, much less about dancing. The Royal Roost and Birdland in Midtown offered modern jazz on that principle,[21] while traditional jazz was played every weekend in cavernous Downtown catering establishments like the Stuyvesant Casino and the Central Plaza; Willie "the Lion" Smith made his appearance once again. Such barn-like places did not offer the attractions of the small clubs, but they were viable for a time.

Throughout the preceding years, the musicians, playing for one another and for audiences in small places, had gradually turned jazz into a listening music. There was very little room to dance in the shoe box clubs on 52nd Street, and it called for a sophisticated artist to dance to bop. The popularity of swing dance bands declined after the war, partly because of a tax on dance floors that the federal government was slow to repeal; when popular dancing revived in the fifties, it was being done to pop songs and rhythm and blues, primarily through recordings.[22]

By that time, jazz music was to be found all over town. Harlem continued to be a center, although most white patrons did not know it because they hardly went there anymore. But Monroe's was open at a new location, as well as Minton's, which continued to have Monday night jam sessions where young musicians went to learn the art. Peter LaRoca Sims remembers playing drums there with clarinetist Tony Scott and bassist Jimmy Garrison in about 1959.

During much of the 52nd Street period, jazz had been played

in Greenwich Village. Cafe Society, where the owners set out to demolish the Jim Crow that prevailed in many clubs, offered swing and boogie-woogie piano. Nick's at Seventh Avenue and 10th Street, and later Eddie Condon's club offered Dixieland. Finally, modern jazz began to take hold in the neighborhood. The Village Vanguard on Seventh Avenue began to gravitate to a consistent music policy.

The most characteristic places, apart from the Vanguard, were the Five Spot and, somewhat later, the Half Note. Both were neighborhood bars on the outer edges of the Village, family businesses that were taken over by young men fresh out of the army; Joe Termini and his brother Iggy at the Five Spot, and Mike Cantarino and his brother Sonny at the Half Note. Although the places were small—just "joints"—the rents were low, and they could afford to put in a little music. A young pianist and French horn player, David Amram, often played at the Five Spot in the mid-fifties.

Although both sets of proprietors later opened larger places— the Terminis briefly ran the Jazz Gallery and another version of the Five Spot on St. Marks Place, and the Cantarinos moved the Half Note uptown to 54th Street—they were less successful; it was the small places that had the attraction. Furthermore, the low rents at the original locations, which are not usual in the history of New York jazz clubs, undoubtedly helped to account for the success and longevity of these two places.[23]

The Five Spot, originally on the Bowery at Cooper Square, became a jazz place in response to demand from local artists, chiefly abstract expressionists. For them, modern jazz had a special meaning; it was an arena of spontaneity, even ecstasy in creation.[24] And indeed, revolutions were made there; Cecil Taylor, Thelonious Monk and Ornette Coleman came to fame playing at the Five Spot. It officially accommodated only seventy-five people, so everyone was close to the music. Nevertheless, it always had two groups, giving younger players a chance to be heard in the relief band. When I asked Joe Termini how it was possible to support all that music, he laughed. "Nobody had money in those days. The rents weren't as high as they are now, and 802 gave us a low scale—seventy-six dollars a week for a sideman, ninety for a leader. The Monk quartet got eight hundred a week. That was a lot for us."[25]

For me, it was the place where I stopped being a moldy fig and began to like modern music, mostly through Monk. One of the originators of bop, having been the house pianist at Minton's, Monk had long roots in more traditional Harlem styles, which perhaps made it possible for me to bridge my gap to the music. I sat through many a set in 1958, glassy-eyed, learning how to listen; it was important to be so close as to be almost inside the music. The experience is quite different from that of listening to classical or big-band, or any music that is planned and familiar. It is like a brilliant conversation on a theme, conducted in a foreign language, in which new ideas are introduced, sometimes dropped and sometimes pursued in a way that the listener can follow if he really listens. The results, when they are recorded, are often less interesting than the process of hearing and seeing the making of the music, because original improvised music strongly conveys the "aura," the sense of awe in the presence of authenticity, of which Walter Benjamin writes.[26] When the music is recorded, nevertheless, its influence can be tremendous. I remember stumbling out of the Five Spot after a searing solo by saxophonist Johnny Griffin on Monk's "Rhythm-a-Ning," only to hear it later on a Riverside live recording, and still later to hear versions of it pour out of the saxophones of younger players.

Musicians liked to play in such places, even though the pay was not very good, in part because the proprietors were honest and appreciative. According to Mike Cantarino, he was able to get Lenny Tristano to come out of his house and play at the Half Note after having shunned clubs for years, because he persuaded Tristano that he was genuinely interested, partly by the purchase of a Bechstein grand piano.[27] I remember Cantarino trying to get noisy people in the audience to keep quiet and listen. On one occasion when Mingus was there with his Jazz Workshop, as the talk grew too loud, Mingus stopped the band (which he did all the time anyhow in order to replay passages) and suddenly switched on the radio to a pop music station. "The contract says music—here it is," Mingus rasped. The customers fell silent, the radio was turned off, and the Jazz Workshop went back to work. I find it hard to picture musicians feeling free to do such a thing except in clubs like these. The arrival of people like Cantarino and the Terminis was a sign that the influence of the "wiseguys" in the jazz business was waning.

In the sixties, the entire club business shifted. The splashy nightclubs with floor shows suffered a slump, causing Max Gordon of the Village Vanguard to say, "Older people have stopped going to clubs and the younger people are going to different places than they used to go."[28] Indeed they were; at the very time the club owners were crying the blues, the City was trying to shut down coffeehouses all over Greenwich Village that had sprung up to offer new kinds of entertainment, including poetry, folk songs and some rock music.[29]

But not much jazz. The music changed radically in the sixties, especially through the influence of the John Coltrane quartet, with McCoy Tyner on piano, Elvin Jones on drums, and Jimmy Garrison or Reggie Workman on bass. Coltrane played a music very different from bop, drawing heavily on elements of African and Eastern music. But the popularity of the music, always marginal, was at a low ebb, overshadowed by rock and folk music. Mike Cantarino remembers one night in the late sixties when the Downtown Half Note, with a big band led by trumpeter Clark Terry, took in six dollars.

The jazz scene in Harlem weakened still further, especially after the riot in the summer of 1964. Black patrons commonly went Downtown for music; in fact the status of Harlem as a center for black business generally was in decline. The owner of the building at 135th and Seventh Avenue that housed Small's on the first floor, when it was going to seed, once said to me, "this place is a casualty of integration." Nevertheless, the Uptown clubs were tenacious. When I went to work in a neighborhood law office in Harlem in 1965, Minton's and Small's were operating, as well as another club for dancing, the Celebrity Club on 125th Street. I went there one night, and found a huge basement dance floor with a bar along one side; Buddy Tate's band was playing and hundreds were dancing. At another little place, the Purple Manor, I was amazed to find a mixed crowd listening to Tiny Grimes, the guitarist, who was then just a name to me from the stories about 52nd Street. From one point of view, the Harlem clubs showed more staying power than any others in Manhattan. A very large percentage of the audience for jazz has always consisted of blacks, and they were keeping at least some of the music in the neighborhood.[30]

Interest revived a little in the seventies. The Angry Squire, a small, dark bar in Chelsea, began to offer jazz, and places started to open on the Upper West Side. Phil Schaap managed the music room at the West End Bar, across from Columbia University, as a place to spark new interest in small-band swing, and Mikell's, a bar at 97th and Amsterdam, began to offer music. Downtown, where musicians were trying to absorb Coltrane's legacy and express entirely new ideas, energetic, experimental music— called simply "loft jazz"—was being played, especially in informal clubs started in the lofts that had opened up to artists. Many of them were run by musicians, including Sam Rivers who had a place called the Studio Rivbea, and the drummer Rashid Ali, who started Ali's Alley. Rivers' place was in a narrow building on Bond Street. In the basement, late in the evening, he played epic sets with his drummer Barry Altschul lasting more than an hour, first playing tenor sax, then flute, often humming or singing along with it, and then playing piano. A band of younger musicians would then play, but Rivers' music was so overpowering that I could barely take in what they did.[31] A somewhat more club-like location for the avant-garde music was the Tin Palace, on the Bowery near the original location of the Five Spot.

Loft jazz has never completely disappeared, although it has thinned out a great deal in the past ten years because of rising rents and noise complaints. Rivers' landlady, a woman of means who fancied herself a painter, once told me that she meant to get rid of him. It did not endear her to me.

By the eighties, there were a handful of established, licensed jazz clubs, including the Village Vanguard and Sweet Basil on Seventh Avenue and Greenwich Village, Fat Tuesdays on Third Avenue, and the one most often found with the famous names and the highest prices, the Blue Note on West Third Street. Most of the clubs, whether established or not, were small and more economically marginal than ever because rents had risen. The hours that the music was played grew shorter, and the custom of having a second "relief" band largely passed away. But the tradition of the way the music is played and shared did not die out. Musicians still came to sit in, and got together to play in joints, some known and some unknown. The Blue Note started having a separate band after the last set of its regular show. During those years, the Burgundy Cafe, like many other little places, opened and closed, a mere wink of an eye in the history of the music. Harlem music was at a low ebb; the New York Swing Dance Society revived lindy-hopping at Small's Paradise just before the place closed for good after some sixty years.

Many of the clubs were and still are more cautious in their booking policies than the jazz lofts used to be; less experimental music is to be heard except in Downtown places like the Knitting Factory. On the other hand, relations between jazz musicians and the rest of the music world had improved. Classical musicians were interested in improvisation, and the New School began to award a bachelor of fine arts degree in its program of jazz and contemporary music.

It was during this period that Local 802 began to move against long-standing restrictions on the clubs, and the City began its "crackdown" on unlicensed establishments.

CHAPTER 4

REGULATION AS DENIGRATION

Once there were real cabarets in New York City. Long before the First World War and the appearance of jazz in the City, there were places with dining and song, and dancing for the patrons. As Lewis Erenberg tells us, they were among the first places of public resort for the upper-middle classes as they emerged from the world of private parties where they had found their social life during the Victorian period.[1]

The cabaret was a curious hybrid of restaurant and theater, where the patrons themselves could participate, at least through dancing. The idea was borrowed from the cabarets of Paris, and lent legitimacy by the connection. Before them there had been palatial restaurants in New York, sometimes with music to accompany dining; but no one who had ever heard the term in those early days would have mistaken restaurants with music for cabarets. Although cabarets were considered bohemian by the standards of the day, because they were "meeting place[s] of the sexes in the eager pursuit of pleasure," theirs was a very staid, not to say swell and expensive, bohemia.[2] Nevertheless, for those who had until recently been part of the reserved Victorian world, they were thought wicked enough. Reisenweber's, where jazz music was first introduced to the city as another novelty (although it had appeared before without a naughty name), was one of them.

In their original form, cabarets were not regulated by the City at all. There was no category for them. As long as they did not use a stage and scenery, and the patrons were gathered at tables as in a restaurant, the cabarets did not, the courts ruled, require a theater license.[3] And indeed, they were not theaters; the relation between the performers and the audience was more informal and intimate than that of a theater.

By the time the City got around to regulating the "cabarets," in 1926, they were gone, destroyed by Prohibition. When the City finally passed a licensing ordinance, it was regulating speakeasies, some of which were no doubt as elegant as the famous cabarets, although more were, as we have seen, just "joints" with music and dancing. In the cabaret law, the City was seeking to apply its regulation to a genre that was already out of date, as it has done consistently from that day to this.

In 1960, during an important cabaret-law scandal, the *New York Post* interviewed Elmer Rogers, a lawyer who had helped to draft the original ordinance. He said, "To understand why this was enacted, you must recall that during Prohibition better than 90 per cent of the speakeasies were controlled by racketeers." He told how Texas Guinan, a famous proprietor of speakeasies, had opened one next to a church, forcing the outraged parishioners to encounter revellers leaving the place on Sunday morning. When the City could not get the owners of nightclubs to police themselves, the ordinance was drafted.[4]

It is apparent, though, that the City's animus ran deeper. The Board of Alderman's Committee on Local Laws was candid about its reasons:

> Your committee gave two public hearings on this bill and its adoption was urged by the police and license commissioners, by clergymen of various denominations and citizens interested in social and recreational work. It was opposed by licensees and owners of cabarets, personally and by their attorneys, and by representatives of musical organizations.
>
> These night clubs or cabarets are simply dance halls,

where food is served at exorbitant prices to the tune of jazz and tabloid entertainment. A very frank opposition was voiced by one of the licensees, on the ground that when strangers came to New York they wanted to 'run Wild.' Well, there has been altogether too much running 'wild' in some of these nightclubs and in the judgment of your committee the 'wild' stranger and the foolish native should have the check-rein applied a little bit. It is well known that the 'wild' strangers are not at all interested in our great museums of art and history, in our magnificent churches and public libraries, our splendid parks and public monuments. They are interested in speakeasies and dance halls and return to their native heaths to slander New York.

Your committee believes that those 'wild' people should not be tumbling out of these resorts at six or seven o'clock in the morning to the scandal and annoyance of decent residents on their way to daily employment.

Favorable action is recommended.[5]

And it was forthcoming. According to the ordinance, a cabaret license was required for:

any room, place or space in the city in which any musical entertainment, singing, dancing or other similar amusement is permitted in connection with the restaurant business or the business of directly or indirectly selling the public food or drink.[6]

The ordinance naturally threw together dancing and music in clubs because at that time the music was always played for dancing. Elmer Rogers later complained of a significant exception in the law, which he thought was "class legislation:" it exempted places of entertainment in large hotels.[7] While this was probably the result of successful lobbying by the hotels, it emphasized the City's intention to control what was not "respectable."

The ordinance must have been largely directed at the black music and dance that was performed in the Harlem clubs, as well as the social mixing of races that was part of "running wild," because in 1926, the "jazz" about which the aldermen complained was being played mostly in Harlem. The aldermen were legislating in the shadow of the view, then widely received throughout the country, that the origin of jazz music and dance in black culture was a source of moral degradation. The distinguished actress Laurette Taylor, starring a hit Broadway play of 1922, *The National Anthem*, which depicted the "saturnalia" produced by jazz, was quoted saying solemnly, "Jazz, the impulse for wildness that has undoubtedly come over many things besides the music of this country, is traceable to the negro influence." In the same year the Illinois Vigilance Association attributed to jazz the "downfall" of one thousand women in Chicago.[8]

The definition of "cabaret," already anachronistic in 1926, was to remain virtually unchanged until 1961, when it was amended to allow live "incidental musical entertainment," but only by a trio of keyboard and strings. The vein of social control enunciated so unmistakably dominated the regulations for more than sixty years; they were, in fact, to become still more restrictive.

THE CABARET IDENTIFICATION CARDS— 1940–1967

The original ordinance regulated only the licensing of the clubs themselves; over the years, it would take on accretions of zoning and safety provisions. In 1931, the administration of the licensing alone, apart from the zoning and safety functions, was transferred from the City's Department of Licenses to the police, who turned it into an instrument of control over the employees of the cabarets. In 1940, the police began to fingerprint every person who worked in a licensed place, and to issue identification cards, denying the cards to people they thought were not of good character. It was unlawful for a club to hire a person who did not have one of the cards, which were renewable every two years.

This administrative measure was to crowd the problems of the club-licensing system entirely out of public consciousness for many years. Maxwell Cohen, a lawyer who crusaded for the elimination of the cards in the fifties, thought that it was originally an anti-radical measure:

> There was around 1939 a Presidential Directive to the FBI instructing them to prepare a list of those whose presence might be adverse to the security of the United States. It was thought that many of the unions were dominated by Communists, particularly the waiters' union. The list was prepared. Later when the police department was helping in an attempt to break a strike, they became involved in passing on the qualifications of waiters and chefs to work in the restaurants. If they had any previous criminal offense, even as minors, they could not work. This was seen as a way of weakening the unions.[9]

The waiters' union certainly agreed. Represented by the Boudin firm, with the New York Civil Liberties Union as *amicus curiae* the union sued to eliminate the fingerprinting and identity cards on the ground that they were beyond the power of the Police commissioner. The state courts did not have much difficulty upholding the regulations, which were to remain in one form or another for over twenty-five years. The justification relied on by the courts, and by every other official who dealt with the issue in succeeding years, had nothing to do with radicals, but rather with the effort to curb corrupting influences on the patrons of those intimate places, the clubs, by preventing ". . . the employment of criminals and other undesirables in cabarets who come in contact with patrons under conditions conducive to criminality. . . ." There actually was a provision in the state

Alcoholic Beverage Control Law, enacted after Prohibition, that forbade the employment in a bar of anyone convicted of a felony or certain other offenses, including narcotics crimes.[10] The racist impulse to control the supposedly degrading abandon of black music was thus absorbed into a vaguer purpose, more acceptable to contemporary tastes, of shielding patrons from "undesirable" influences.

Undoubtedly there was some underworld involvement in running the clubs—that was one of the things that made it hard to enjoy working in them. But the nexus between crime and the musicians and other entertainers was entirely symbolic. Neither the news reports nor the cases reveal a single instance during the entire controversy when anyone, whether from the police or any other source, claimed that a musician, or any entertainer, was denied a card because he had committed a crime in or even close to a club. The cards were invariably denied because of a past criminal record, often for narcotics offenses.

The musicians and their fans experienced the requirement of an identity card as a denigration of their work. Most notorious was the case of Billie Holiday, who was denied a cabaret card after a major narcotics conviction and a prison term in 1947.[11] From the City's point of view the denial is actually easy to understand because hers was a scandalous case; she might even have provoked action by the State Liquor Authority if she had been hired in a New York club. But for jazz fans, it only served to underline the fact that the state and City authorities were concerned with her criminal record, and not at all with her artistry; that she was one of the very greatest of singers, at least in the period before the jail term, seemed to make no difference to the city or state authorities at all. This interpretation, however, seems to me to oversimplify what the City was doing; although city officials did denigrate the work of such an artist, they did not do it blindly. They must have recognized and feared the power of the work, even if they denied it. Otherwise why bother to control it?

The regulation was made to seem still more hypocritical by

the fact that Billie Holiday, or any other artist, could sing in other places—in a theater, or even at a concert in Central Park, as Holiday did in 1948 and later years. But theaters and even concerts in the park are not intimate places; this characteristic of the regulation suggests that one of its functions was to prevent any close contact between the audience and the seductive art and supposedly seductive life of Billie Holiday and at least to control contact with others who practiced the abandoned arts of these nightclubs.

In any case, the regulation successfully degraded the status of working in a club; the musicians and others experienced it just that way. Comedian Joey Adams, the head of the American Guild of Variety Artists, said "Why do performers have to be treated like gangsters? New York is the only city that has this licensing requirement. . . . Why do we have to be fingerprinted and mugged, and not prizefighters and their managers, for instance?"[12]

The way the police administered the regulations dramatized the status-degradation through a pervasive atmosphere of personal influence and petty graft. Musicians were sent to the photo studio next door to the license office to pay for an identification photo even if they had brought a photo with them.[13] Some people who were denied a card at first found they could hire a lawyer, get a hearing and eventually get a card. Maxwell Cohen said that the ". . . hearings were usually before an inspector who was sympathetic. They were simple hearings. I would produce the applicant and he would testify that he was married and that he had not committed an offense for a number of years. In other words, that he was rehabilitated. . . ."[14] Very important artists, like Sonny Stitt, a leading altoist following Charlie Parker, and Bud Powell, the fountainhead of bop piano, were eventually able to get cards only through police hearings.[15]

Yet some musicians found that they could not get a card at all, or did not get one for years, perhaps because they did not know how or had no money to fight the problem. In some cases, the system made a material difference to the history of the music.

Thelonious Monk lost his card in 1951, when he was arrested in an auto with Bud Powell; the story was that heroin was found at Monk's feet. Monk, who notoriously found it difficult to deal with non-musical life, took the rap, lost his cabaret card, and did not devise a way to get it back for six years. The bassist Buell Neidlinger recalls seeing Monk playing at a West Indian dance during this time as a way of making a little money. Monk was able to get his card in 1957, according to a biography, "with the help of influential friends."[16] It was then that Monk, after being a subterranean bop master for over fifteen years, began to exert his full influence by launching his famous quartet at the Five Spot. It was little wonder that an unnamed musician told George Hoefer of *Downbeat*, "Everybody knows you can buy a police card if you have money and the right connections. Look at the guys with police records who are working New York clubs and then look at the lesser known musicians who are not working because they don't have the money or influence."[17]

In my view, the requirement of a cabaret card influenced the music in more subtle ways. To play jazz was to be a musical outsider, even sometimes a revolutionary, to cut against the grain of ordinary musical taste. The City's rules governing the lives of musicians, together with the nature of the places where the music was played, only exemplified, indeed legislated, that status. And many musicians lived the status, making it a part of them. If they played complex and difficult music, and played it as they pleased, they paid the price for it. They rejected and were rejected by the "square" world.

In the late fifties, the clamor against the cabaret cards began to rise. Maxwell Cohen brought a suit to test once again the identity-card requirement, using bandleader Johnny Richards, together with two of his side musicians, pianist Bill Rubenstein, and trombonist J.J. Johnson as plaintiffs. The facts presented sobering examples of the arbitrariness of the regulations. Once convicted of a marijuana offense, Rubenstein had been twice denied a card after police hearings. From an artistic point of view, the denial to J.J. Johnson was even more dismaying. The indispensable master of modern-jazz trombone, without whose work the City was much poorer artistically, Johnson had been once caught with a hypodermic thirteen years earlier. The court awarded the cards, but the system remained undisturbed.[18]

Local 802 successfully lobbied for a state bill that deprived the New York City police of the power to deny a card if the person was acceptable under the standards of the State Liquor Authority. But by this time the City had solidified the ideology which justified the regulations by the supposed corrupting influences of its clubs; Governor Rockefeller vetoed the bill in 1959 after the mayor appealed to him to do so because of what the police commissioner called the "peculiar problems in New York City concerning cabarets."[19]

The attack came to a head at the end of 1960 in a protracted squabble that dramatized the degrading underside of the system of regulation, as well as its resilience as a system of control. It began when an influential writer, Harold Humes, persuaded Joe Termini to hire Richard "Lord" Buckley for a stint at the Jazz Gallery on St. Marks Place. Lord Buckley was a "hip" comedian, who combined references to the classics in dialect monologues; one of his famous ones, about Jesus Christ, was called "The Naz" (short for "The Nazarene"). Buckley applied for and received a cabaret card, without admitting that he had once been arrested for marijuana, and once convicted for drunkenness. When the police picked up his record from the fingerprint check, they went to the Jazz Gallery and ordered him to leave the stage, without even giving him a chance to finish his monologue.

Buckley tried to use influence to get the card, but then died suddenly of a stroke. Incensed, Humes organized leading writers and entertainers into a Citizens Emergency Committee to put an end to the card system. They charged that there was corruption and preferential treatment in its administration. Specifically, they said, Buckley had been told that he could get in the good graces of the police department if he performed at an Honor Legion dinner, an unofficial occasion. And he had done so.[20]

That was astounding enough in itself; here was a man supposed to be *persona non grata* in New York night life, invited to perform at a police function. The idea, as I see it, was that one could be a performer, but only if one's outlawry were made safe by authority, only if one became a creature of the police system of regulation. There is a similar story about Billie Holiday, that once in the Five Spot she was asked to "sit in" and sing, although she could not do so as an employee. Because a police captain was present, she at first refused, until Joe Termini said, "He'd love to hear you." She sang, for the moment accepting the fact that she could do so only at the sufferance of the police.[21]

But there was more. The Citizens Emergency Committee claimed that at the Honor Legion dinner where Buckley performed, a theatrical agent told him that he could get the card for a hundred dollars from a Deputy Commissioner. This charge was denied by the agent named, but was substantiated by a witness to the exchange. More sensationally, the Citizens Committee also claimed that Frank Sinatra had worked in New York clubs in the fifties without a cabaret card. The Police Commissioner, after first rashly denying that it was possible, found that Sinatra had repeatedly worked at the Copacabana. Sinatra was quoted saying, "I will not seek a cabaret card in New York because of the indignity of being fingerprinted, mugged and quizzed about my past."[22]

There was a huge publicity scandal, of the sort that the newspapers love because it involves celebrities; it was on the front pages for days.[23] Entertainment unions, including the musicians', called on the governor to investigate, and he in turn asked Mayor Wagner for a report. Police Commissioner Stephen Kennedy ordered an intensive investigation of all cabarets, in order—repeating the pious litany—"to prevent their becoming a rendezvous of criminals and persons of questionable character."[24] One thousand policemen inspected 2,478 places just before Thanksgiving, when the impact of a raid upon holiday trade was at a maximum. What they revealed was a grotesque evasion of the regulations. The famous torch singer Sophie Tucker and her accompanist were working without cards in a fancy club; in every major place, in fact, people were found to be working without them.

The Citizens Committee complained that all this outcry about lax enforcement was beside the point; what they were after was no enforcement. At the end of November 1960, Maxwell Cohen began another lawsuit in the state Supreme Court against the cabaret-card system, this one brought by singer Nina Simone, composer-arranger Quincy Jones, the Village Gate night club, and some dissidents in the musicians union. But they should have foreseen that when they attacked a bureaucracy, especially by impugning its honesty, they were sure to get a bureaucratic response. This one came in the form of a crackdown. The licenses for expensive clubs, including the Copacabana, the Stork Club and El Morocco, were suspended. Joey Adams, who, like Sinatra, had refused to apply for a card, was forced to get one; in a variation on his earlier comment, he was quoted saying, "Why should we have to get police permission to work any more than the guys in the dress business or newspaper reporters? If even an ex-convict has paid his debt to society and is law-abiding, I don't see why he as to pay a bribe to somebody in order to be allowed to play a horn or dance in a nightclub."[25]

The moral that any observant musician would draw was that those with power and money did not comply with the rules; It was only marginalized chumps like Lord Buckley and the jazz musicians who would be forced to comply, so that they would understand in what low esteem they and their haunts were held.

The results of this publicity fire storm were strangely thin; it had been a lot of sound and fury signifying social control. The posh clubs got their licenses back in court, and the mayor reported no substantial evidence of corruption. At the beginning of 1961, he announced that the identity cards of entertainers and musicians would be made permanent, rather than renewable, and that the administration would be transferred to the Department of Licenses. Police Commissioner Kennedy pronounced himself delighted; he only wished the mayor would take taxi licensing off his hands as well.[26] It seemed that the Commissioner had never liked the job of policing the cabarets, probably because he recognized the likelihood of corruption. But nothing was done about the denial to musicians of their ability to work based on their records; as if to put a period to the scandal, Nina Simone's case was dismissed on the authority of the old waiters' union case.[27] The court thus reinforced the policy of using the cabaret cards to control corrupting influences.

The reason for these minimal results after two years of agitation were characteristic of New York. The power to make a definitive change was diffused, split between the state and the City. More important, there was no real power, either from public pressure or elsewhere, in favor of the change; much influential opinion in fact favored the social control over cabaret employees. The *New York Times* editorialized in support of the cabaret cards, saying "A system of surveillance that keeps the underworld from getting into the nightclub business is a protection to the public and to the decent people who prevail in the dining-with-entertainment industry."[28] And the director of the Citizens Union, in expressing his approval of the system of identity cards, laid bare the underlying fears with surgical precision:

> Intimacy is encouraged by the crowding, the drinking, the music and the dim lights. . . . In such surroundings, a shady character can make hay while the sun is not shining.[29]

No wonder the governor had vetoed the musicians union's bill in 1959; the wonder is that it was passed in the first place.

There were some straws of change in the wind. During the early sixties, the *New York Times* and other establishment media began to take the popular arts more seriously, reviewing and reporting them regularly. In the spring of 1961, John Lindsay, then congressman from the so-called silk-stocking district of New York and later to be mayor, in commenting on the transfer of jurisdiction over clubs to the Department of Licenses added that "requiring work permits is an unreasonable exercise of the city's police power."[30]

But the end was not yet; one of the most significant and ironic of the cabaret-card cases occurred in 1961. Buell Neidlinger, then a well-known young bass player in New York, noted for his work with pianist Cecil Taylor, lost his card after the stereotypical marijuana arrest. Neidlinger was not your typical jazz musician; he was a classically trained string player, who had attended Yale for a year. Something of a prodigy, he had become fascinated with jazz. What had happened to him was the nightmare of the policy-makers who sought to control the life of the clubs: he had been pulled into that wild music and that life. But he did not have to stay in it; he left New York to play in the Houston Symphony, the Boston Symphony and finally to teach and play on the West Coast. The symphony orchestras, not to speak of the listening public, surely would not have thought of an arrest as in any way relevant to his work and the municipal authorities would not have presumed to inquire. Contact with the audience even for chamber music was dignified, if not distant, and the music, while it might be impassioned in a refined way, was not part of that low life the authorities identified with jazz.

Neidlinger sees the significance of these events acutely. "I was lucky," he told me. "I did not have to suffer the way a lot of others did when I lost my card." He later got it back through a hearing, represented by Maxwell Cohen, he says, for a fee of a thousand dollars. But he never came back to New York. In the sixties he said, "The American situation for jazz is the most miserable that I have ever seen. And it's not getting any better. Now that I don't make my living from it anymore, I can see it quite objectively, and I think it's getting worse." In 1990 he still says "I need jazz like a hole in the head"—but he would like to play a gig in New York.[31]

When John Lindsay came into office as mayor in 1966, he brought with him an attitude to popular culture, to urban life both indoors and out, that was different from that of his prede-cessors. His election was the break between the free-and-easy, rights-oriented spirit of the later sixties and the staid attitudes of the earlier decades. He and his cohorts sought to make New York "Fun City," partly no doubt to encourage the tourist trade, but also because they were less suspicious of fun, and of the diversity of the City. They made it a little easier, for example, for sidewalk cafes to open, and they determined to get rid of the hated fingerprinting and then the cabaret cards.[32]

It proved to be as easy for the City administration to eliminate them as it had been difficult for outsiders like Lord Buckley and Harold Humes to do so. After trying to get the City Council to pass a bill to abolish fingerprinting, the administration realized that none was needed. The fingerprinting had begun as the result of an administrative decision in 1940, and could be ended the same way; Mayor Lindsay simply ordered it to be ended. That somehow broke the spell of fear of wicked comedians and musi-cians; the rest was simple. The *New York Times* editorialized in praise of that decision and of one to permit poetry readings in Washington Square. When the bill to ratify the mayor's action by eliminating the licensing of club employees came up in the City Council, the License Commissioner scoffed at the notion ". . . that the safety of the public is served by a system which presupposes a need to be suspicious of everyone, from top-flight artists [to] go-go girls and bartenders, and require them to submit to the indignity of a police-like check." The bill passed with only one vote in opposition.[33]

The abolition of the cabaret cards was a curious example of a change in social attitudes and administrative practice, without a clear-cut change in legal norms. The card system simply disap-peared, as a hated symbol of a repressive past; and yet it is to this day not completely clear that the use of the identity cards with its accompanying character test would be unconstitutional, even under contemporary law. The bar to employment in the state Alcoholic Beverage Control law still remains, for example, but there is no machinery for enforcement. It continues in the law like an appendix in the body, potentially dangerous but having lost its function.[34]

THE LICENSING OF CLUBS—
1926–1986

The entire system of cabaret cards was supposed to have been ancillary to the control of the clubs themselves; the regulation of the clubs drew on the same apprehensions because it was the clubs, after all, that were supposed to be crime-ridden and filled with temptations. Nevertheless, the problems of getting or losing a license to run a club never carried the emotional power of getting or losing a license to play in one. It seemed to be a commercial drama rather than a personal and artistic one, at least until we brought our lawsuit in 1986 on behalf of the musicians, and against the club-licensing.

The control purposes and functions of club licensing were so much a part of daily municipal regulation that they were almost invisible. In part they were bound up in the technical details of the application for and maintenance of the license. But if the club owners had been required to do no more than get and renew a license, harassing as that might have been, they would not have experienced such persistent difficulties. Their chief problem lay in the combination of licensing and zoning regulations.

By the time of the 1926 cabaret-licensing ordinance, New York had been regulating the use of land for ten years; zoning had come to seem one of the quintessential municipal functions. Zoning was and is one of the areas in which a city government has enormously broad discretion to express its value judgements, even its prejudices, about business and pleasure in various parts of the city. For one thing, zoning can be a powerful means of hiding away and even excluding uses that the municipality finds dangerous, fearful or exotic. The zoning regulations could be used, for example, to shunt jazz and other music into "districts" like 52nd Street. When the owners of the Street wanted it for other purposes, and contrived to use the licensing regulations to eliminate the clubs, music could be channeled into manufacturing districts, to which listeners would have to make a pilgrimage at night.

More importantly, the zoning of places of entertainment was independent of their licensing, and centered in a different city agency. The combination of zoning and licensing thus created a double barrier to clubs, of which zoning was the more difficult to hurdle. Bars and restaurants were compelled to get a license, but if they were not in the proper zone, they were not eligible for the license except through special dispensation. (See chart at the end of the book). This dispersion of the problem throughout different city agencies was poorly understood by would-be reformers.

ON TRYING NOT TO BE A CABARET

Over the years, bars, restaurants and cafes sought to narrow the interpretation of a "cabaret" under the 1926 regulation, in an effort to exempt themselves from the licensing requirements. And it is in the disputes about what was and was not a cabaret that clues to the municipal purpose emerge.

Jazz music and dancing were largely separate by the fifties, when the music was fading from 52nd Street. The character of bars and restaurants that had music only for listening had changed, diverging from that of dancing spots, which were big halls, like Roseland, posh nightclubs, or depressed taxi-dance halls. The jazz clubs were small joints, occasionally spruced up but fairly basic, sometimes with decent food but in essence dedicated to listening and playing. Yet the cabaret-licensing scheme continued to bracket together music and dancing. The effect was that a restaurant that had any live music at all was required to get a cabaret license, and more importantly, was zoned out of many places where plain restaurants were legal. The proprietors of those true cabarets from before the First

World War would have been amazed to learn what the City now thought was a cabaret.

In 1955, Local 802 of the musicians union, after years of lobbying, took a stumbling step toward getting the City to recognise the separation of music from dancing, although not toward accommodating the jazz clubs. Particularly galled by a provision in the Zoning Resolution that permitted only canned music in restaurants outside the zones where entertainment was permitted, the officers of the Local persuaded the mayor and the City Planning Commission to adopt a zoning amendment permitting up to three musicians, playing strings or keyboards, to play in restaurants. The union was hoping to snare jobs for string and piano trios at posh restaurants on the Upper East Side, while studiously trying to avoid any implication that lower-class music might be encouraged. The amendment was proposed in order to provide employment, the union said, not to interfere with the aims of zoning ". . . to maintain certain standards of peace and quiet in specific areas of the City, and to prevent and discourage congregating by undesirable elements in them."[35]

This measure was very unfriendly to jazz. While jazz can be played using strings and keyboards alone, as can rock music, which was just becoming popular in the mid-fifties, the exclusion of horns and percussion was obviously meant to convey a flavor of classical or subdued cocktail music. If they had been asked, the union's officers probably would have said that the project of releasing jazz from the grip of the zoning exclusions seemed hopeless, and that even a small change that would help a few musicians was better than nothing.

Although I never have seen any comment on the effects of this zoning change, I am persuaded that it made virtually no difference, because Local 802 apparently failed to see how complex the legal change had to be in order to be effective. Although the Board of Estimate, with the participation of the mayor, could change the Zoning Resolution at that time, the old cabaret ordinance administered by the police still required a license for any sort of musical "entertainment." Under the jurisdiction of the City's legislative body, the City Council, it was not to be changed for another six years.

During that period, tastes in entertainment began to shift toward the interests characteristic of the sixties. By 1960, the nightclub business was in the doldrums, while people were flocking to coffee houses, chiefly in Greenwich Village, that offered poetry readings, comedy, theater, and sometimes music. People were in search of places of resort that were still more informal, intimate and bohemian than those that had gone before. As Village residents began to complain about them, the police began to issue summonses to the coffee houses as unlicensed cabarets. There were a lot of them by contemporary standards; in May of 1961, the *New York Times* reported that sixty summonses were pending against coffeehouses, and in 1964, fifteen unlicensed coffeehouses that offered entertainment were ordered closed.[36]

The coffeehouse owners tried to avoid the strictures of the zoning and licensing laws by claiming that they were culturally different from cabarets; they did not serve liquor and did not offer "entertainment" in the honky-tonk sense. The criminal courts sometimes accepted the claim, made repeatedly, that reading poetry was not "entertainment," although the police went right on issuing summonses.[37] Music presented a more interesting and complex problem; the extraordinary case of the Cafe Figaro created the sharpest possible contrast between the treatment, social as well as legal, of the classical and the vernacular. The situation arose in the 1950's when one of New York's Renaissance men, Stefan Bauer-Mengelberg, was making a transition to a career as a symphony conductor, while teaching mathematics at New York University in Washington Square. During that period he became a regular at the Figaro, a coffeehouse on the corner of Bleecker and MacDougal Streets run by one of his students, Tom Ziegler. Mr. Bauer-Mengelberg, now a lawyer with a strong interest in the arts who edits the mathematical works of Gödel in his spare time, recalls:

Ziegler was not much interested in the arts or in literature. . . . but he had a sense of what a coffeehouse should be like. And he felt that coffeehouses should be putting on performances and that they should supply their customers with foreign newspapers to read and things of that kind. . . .

When Ziegler decided that he wanted to have a musical program, he asked me to sort of supervise the organisation of it. . . . I found a very able clarinetist, Saul Kurtz, with whom I had participated in performances—a very good musician, fine instrumentalist and very well connected in the New York pool of players—and I persuaded Saul to take on the job of actually organising the concerts in detail.

I think it is important in connection with the cabaret law to relate the concerns that I discussed with Tom Ziegler about the nature of these performances. I was not interested in being involved in a music program that would simply provide background music to restaurant activity. I extracted from Tom the promise—which was very gladly and freely given; he was quite serious about this—that these would really be concerts, concerts in a coffeehouse setting, as they might have taken place in the time of Bach. . . . So that it was agreed that when the performance had started, the table service would stop. . . . Moreover, we decided that the concerts should be absolutely free. . . . It was non-commercial to a "T."

The next problem was to get players of the kind of quality that we wanted to have appear there. Initially they were very "offish," and said, "Oh, who wants to play in a restaurant?" and so on. Once a player had played in the Figaro, we couldn't keep him away. We were besieged by questions, "When can I come again?". . . . They absolutely loved it, because the audience was very serious, it was extraordinarily intimate. Tables would be moved aside to create a small area, so the audience . . .

could practically touch the musicians. . . . It was a remarkable atmosphere, so the players rose to the occasion.[38]

On several occasions, the police served summonses on Ziegler
for running an unlicensed cabaret. He made no attempt to obtain
a license, both because he preferred to resist the bureaucracy, and
because he was unwilling to subject his staff and the musicians to
the indignities of the identification process; it appeared in any
case that his location was not zoned for a cabaret. In 1960 he
mounted an elaborate defense, assisted by a lawyer from the
musicians union, during which Bauer-Mengelberg testified to
the characteristics of the concerts, making the point that this was
not "entertainment"—during the performance, the Cafe Figaro
became a concert hall.

Bauer-Mengelberg's credentials were impressive, to put it
mildly; he was associated both with the New York and the St.
Louis Philharmonics. After the trial was reported in the papers,
he says, "I underwent a great deal of ribbing at the Philharmonic,
because all the people in the orchestra read this article, and the
more conservative ones said, 'What are you doing in this drug
culture?'—there was no drug culture at the Figaro at all. . . ."

In his decision, the magistrate accepted all of Bauer-Mengelberg's arguments, reaching all the way back to the Board of
Aldermen's report of 1926 to note that the Figaro concerts were
just the sort of cultural event that the City fathers had wanted
visitors to attend instead of the jazz and "tabloid" entertainments
of the clubs. He wrote:

> I am convinced that a critical difference exists between a
> cabaret—i.e., a restaurant with dancing and singing as
> entertainment—and Cafe Figaro, a coffee, pastry and
> sandwich restaurant, where an admission-free, Sunday
> afternoon concert of Beethoven, Schubert and Bach-
> Forbes took place on September 18, 1960. Though to the
> Police Department such difference may be impalpable,
> those who came to listen to the Gurevich trio could

hardly have imagined they were in the kind of place that the Municipal Assembly found frequented by " 'wild' strangers."[39]

The Cafe Figaro created an opening through which classical music might have blended with some of the real attractions of a small club. The police, however, would probably not have accepted a "classical music exception" unless they were compelled by a change in the ordinance; in any case, no proprietor except Tom Ziegler ever undertook a program as rigorous as the one Bauer-Mengelberg prescribed.

Even though most of the coffeehouse owners did not offer exclusively poetry or chamber music in a concert format, they searched for ways to escape the regulatory system, sensing that the "cabaret" designation was anachronistic. They pointed out that they did not serve liquor. They accused the police of corruption in the administration of licenses at a time when the police had recently come under similar attack for the administration of the identity cards.[40]

The results of that campaign, however, were as meager as the one against cabaret cards. As part of Mayor Wagner's package at the beginning of 1961 that transferred the administration of club licensing to the Department of Licenses, the City Council finally got around to legislating as a separate licensing ordinance the distinction the musicians union had lobbied into the Zoning Resolution, permitting any restaurant, including a coffeehouse, to have "incidental musical entertainment" by up to three live musicians, provided they played only keyboards and strings. For coffeehouses that wanted to have more substantial entertainment, a special classification was established permitting them to apply for a "coffeehouse license."[41] This mere change of name, from "cabaret" to "coffeehouse" appears to have been something close to a macabre municipal joke. As far as I can tell, it did not even eliminate the hated identity cards; more important, it was, once again, not coordinated with zoning. The Zoning Resolution did not distinguish "coffeehouse" zoning from that of any other place of entertainment; thus such establishments could not legally be started in most of Greenwich Village.

The coffeehouses went on for years violating the licensing laws and getting summonsed. By the mid-sixties, the fight to control coffeehouses was being successfully led by the reform Democratic District leader, Edward Koch, later Mayor Koch, who, together with his co-leader Carol Greitzer, was in a position to put pressure on the City to enforce the ordinances. Even the Lindsay administration, which disliked the cabaret laws and was sympathetic to the coffeehouses, did not prevent their demise as places of entertainment at the end of the sixties.[12]

ON TRYING TO BE A CABARET

It was not surprising that coffeehouses and restaurants with three musicians or less sought to avoid being classified as cabarets, even in those few cases when they happened to be in zones that permitted entertainment. Many of those that, like the jazz clubs, could not avoid the classification, found it daunting to cope with.

The punctilio of the regulations could be used to eliminate clubs when powerful interests sought to banish them. On August 1, 1953, the *New York Times* reported that one side of 52nd Street had been bought, together with the club leases, to be replaced eventually by an office skyscraper. On August 4, the Three Deuces on 52nd Street was raided by the police and its books and permits were seized; on August 8, its license was suspended because it had not been keeping a proper list of employees: two of them turned out to be working without cabaret cards. On the same date, a similar process was begun against a 52nd Street club called the Moulin Rouge.[43] This was, of course, a way of putting the clubs out of business; by implication, moreover, it raised the question of how they had stayed in business so long. It suggested that the regulations were so complicated, or the management so slipshod, that the clubs could continue only at the sufferance of the authorities. The licensing created a complicity between the police and the clubs, giving rise to an atmosphere of corruption in which only "wiseguys" survive—the very situation that was supposed to be one of the problems with the club business.

The licensing process itself was the nemesis of some music clubs, as it has been up to the end of the eighties. Both the Five Spot and the Half Note were located on the periphery of residential neighborhoods, the Five Spot on the Bowery at Cooper Square, between the East and West Villages, and the Half Note at Spring and Hudson Streets, slightly south of Greenwich Village. They were thus in zones that permitted them to obtain cabaret licenses if they could comply with the regulations. At first neither place had any trouble getting a license; they were small, established bars that could continue serving liquor while they waited for the bureaucracy to process their applications; Mike Cantarino of the Half Note says that the local firemen, whom he knew well, told him how to comply with safety requirements.

The Five Spot faced difficulties later. When the club moved to a bigger place three blocks up on St. Marks Place, the Terminis waited for months in the winter of 1962 to '63 for a license; it was during this period that vibraphonist Warren Chiasson, later a plaintiff in the 1986 case, was forced out of his trio with Roland Hanna and Teddy Kotick. After the nightclub business sank into somnolence in the early sixties, the Terminis let their cabaret license lapse while they tried to run the place as a restaurant. When they reapplied for a license in 1974, they were unable to cut through the red tape. They ran the club for months without a license, receiving summonses, and finally closed in 1976. From their account of their problems, it appears that they were unable to coordinate their application through the Fire Department, the Buildings Department and the licensing department itself, by then called the Department of Consumer Affairs.[44]

This is not surprising. Robert Bookman, a lawyer who formerly worked at the Department of Consumer Affairs, finds expediting these applications quite frustrating. Approval for the club—certification that it complies with the building and fire code requirements for cabarets—must be obtained and submitted to the Consumer Affairs Department, which may delay the application for other inspections. Even with Bookman's help, the process takes several months.[45]

The Terminis did not have the help of a Robert Bookman; perhaps they could not have afforded it, or did not realize they needed legal assistance. They were running a small club, and as small businessmen will, they tried to solve their problems themselves. After the place was closed, Iggy Termini said, "We put so much into the Five Spot, so much work and about $100,000, and now it seems almost as if it was nothing." And Joe Termini reflected, "You have to come to terms with the environment. If this were Europe, Iggy and I would be famous and the musicians who work here would be on television every night."[46]

Like the musicians, the Terminis felt that their inability to get a permit reflected at best the City's ignorance and at worst its contempt. They were, in part, the victims of the system, by then already more than twenty years out of date, of bracketing music with dancing for purposes of licensing and zoning. During the years the Five Spot was open, discotheques became fashionable. Imported from France, like the cabarets of fifty years earlier, they signalled the ultimate divorce of dancing and live music. There was money invested in some of the discotheques, and money to be made in them, at least in the short run. Many of them were able to cope, however unhappily, with cabaret licensing, while many of the jazz clubs could not.[47]

The misfortune arose because the licensing authorities, following the law, drew no clear distinction between music-only clubs and discotheques. During the early seventies it became routine for the City, thinking of a typical nightclub as a discotheque, to expect that considerable capital would be tied up in a club, some of which could be spent for lawyers and technical needs. At the same time, the City showed no sympathy or respect for the clubs; they were just a source of revenue, and if they had problems, that was too bad for them. The City's long-standing suspicion of the vernacular arts, combined with cautious tolerance, had become fastened on social dancing. The small bar that wanted to have a little music did not exist for the City administration. The officials seemed unable to imagine that a place that is small and underfinanced could be a major cultural resource, frequented by musicians of the greatest talent.

The corrosive effects of the City's treatment of potential licensees was slowed in the mid-seventies, when the City's fiscal crisis led to budget cuts, particularly in the Department of Consumer Affairs.[48] One of the results, according to some sources, was a practical acceptance of the fact that music clubs were not really cabarets. Inspectors and other enforcement personnel had discretion to relax the code in cases where there was no real nuisance to local people. An informal policy developed of not issuing summonses to places that had no dancing—a "music only" policy—when the places did not provoke complaints from the neighborhood. Phil Schaap, who from 1974 to 1984 managed the music at the West End Bar, across Broadway from Columbia University, recounts his experience of this policy:

> When we first started, the tenant above complained, and Sidney Roberts [the proprietor] called an acoustics expert, who I believe was a professor at Vassar. He came down from Poughkeepsie at fifty dollars an hour and told me what to do. He told me where to drill holes in this man's floor, to air-blow in sound proofing, and he was very specific about the caulking I was to use to seal the holes. . . . I don't really understand what he was telling me to do, but I did exactly what he told me to do. And I remember his bill was for fifty dollars—a one-hour consultancy—which I thought was very cost-effective. I soundproofed that floor, and we never had another complaint.
>
> The fire marshals came in regularly. They didn't seem

to me to be looking to have their palms greased. I found them to be strong, silent types. They walked around, did their business and left. No complaints. No summonses. Then, in January of '78, to accommodate a new piano— we had been using uprights, we brought in a Steinway baby grand—we built an extension to the stage, raising it and extending it. Shortly thereafter . . . a fire marshal came in, and he was quite blunt and serious. He took out a white soap-bar, he marked the stage, and he said "This will be gone tomorrow night at eight o'clock, or I'm going to padlock the place," and split. It was a violation of the fire code, because we cut down the exit— the exit had to be open.

We called a carpenter . . . he cut that corner of the stage off, which made things cramped. The white-capped fire marshal came, he nodded and that was that. . . .

The only time a city official ever came in, related to the cabaret code, was in 1978. . . . I pointed out that we thought we were in compliance—I don't know whether I truly believed that—I said, "When we started, we had a sound problem; we solved it. We never had a problem with the fire department except the one time, and we solved it. We abide by the laws, Columbia's happy and— this is our little neighborhood bar jazz scene." He said, "Okay," and he's gone. There was no question of anything serious going on. I wouldn't even call it an inspection. He said, "Hi. We're checking out your jazz club— you seem to have one on-going." We never, ever had a problem.[49]

It was under these circumstances that experimental jazz was played in musicians' lofts Downtown during the seventies. The places were opened and operated for as long as their proprietors could keep them open. In general, they did not apply for licenses, and the licensing system was not invoked against them.

At the same time, ironically, the technical requirements to obtain a license became more stringent. After a fatal fire in 1975 at the Blue Angel, a midtown nightclub, licensed clubs were required to have special sprinklers, a second exit and other safety devices.[50]

As a result of all these forces, fewer and fewer places were licensed. In 1960, at the height of the scandals concerning police enforcement of the cabaret cards and licenses, newspapers reported that there were eleven or twelve hundred cabaret licensees throughout the five boroughs. By 1986, the Department of Consumer Affairs was to report less than two hundred.[51]

CHAPTER 5

THE CAMPAIGN TO CHANGE THE LAW: LOST IN THE LABYRINTH

THE CRACKDOWN AND THE CLUBS

In the late seventies, when the Department of Consumer Affairs was staying its hand from "music only" clubs, its powers were in fact relatively limited. Consumer Affairs could issue summonses, which were effective against law-abiding people like the Termini brothers, but without a court order it could not close down a recalcitrant scofflaw like a noisy illegal dance hall. In 1982, with the fiscal crisis easing, Consumer Affairs received the power to impose increased fines and to close down clubs through its own administrative processes, without the intervention of a court. In 1984, the City allocated funds for the Department to increase nighttime enforcement; and as one official said, there wasn't a great deal in the way of consumer affairs work to do at night except to check on nightclubs.[1]

The result was systematic and increasing enforcement. Gone was discretion for the inspectors and lawyers to ignore a violation which was considered harmless. The Department began to abandon a long-standing policy of permitting a *bona fide* applicant for a license to operate as a club while the license was pending. Instead, all inspections and papers needed to be completed before a four-piece band would be allowed to play a note. The pattern was to enforce as thoroughly as possible, closing clubs by padlocking their doors when necessary to make the system credible, and collecting substantial fines. Consumer Affairs increased the economic impact by charging a fine as a separate violation for each day that the offending club was open after the inspector first checked it.[2]

Consumer Affairs sometimes justified its policy by pointing out that safety requirements were different for cabarets and for bars and restaurants. The safety requirements had indeed been made more stringent after the Blue Angel fire of 1975, on the theory that patrons in a place of entertainment are less aware of their surroundings because their attention is riveted on the show. The theory, however, had little support either in the Blue Angel experience or anything else.[3]

Some places, having long known about the law permitting only "incidental musical entertainment," had tailored their musical policies to fit, limiting themselves to a singer or at most a trio with piano and strings. Bradley's on University Place had a policy of hiring only duos of piano and bass, and the nearby Knickerbocker followed suit. The three-musician restriction had shaped the music. David Levy, one of the founders of the School of Jazz Studies at the New School, says "I remember when the Mitchell-Ruff duo played at the Hickory House in the fifties. We thought that was an odd idea—just piano and bass. Twenty-five years later it seemed routine, because the smaller places could not use any other instruments." A number of strong and famous piano-bass duos developed, like the partnership of Junior Mance and Marty Rivera. Mance says that he started playing with Rivera and without drums because he found that there were many gigs where he could not play with a drummer.[4] Such music was not "incidental" at all, of course, but the language of the exception did not cast a net fine enough to catch it.

Some of the clubs were sitting ducks for the inspectors. When the West End Bar, on Upper Broadway, and the Angry Squire, on Seventh Avenue near 23rd Street, received summonses in

1986, the owners were astounded. They did not even know that they were in violation of the law. Dan Lynch's and Preacher's, two bars that offered rock and blues, were fined and padlocked. The pianist Barry Harris was running the Jazz Cultural Theater on Eighth Avenue, where he had a music school, a big band for his students, as well as regular concerts for the public. The City added to his many financial woes by giving him summonses for running a cabaret.[5]

Some club owners responded to the stepped-up enforcement by trying to get a cabaret license. Larry Heller, then of the West End Bar, began the slow process, only to find, months later, that the application had not been completed and he could still book only trios. Mel Litoff and his partners from Sweet Basil, a licensed club on Seventh Avenue, took over Lush Life, a place nearby on Bleecker Street, and created a strong jazz club. Peter LaRoca Sims, the drummer-lawyer, among many others, played there and received good notices. The new owners began the process of applying for a cabaret license, such as they had success-fully negotiated for Sweet Basil. But they found this time that they could not qualify. The partners asked some of the bands already booked to cut themselves down to trios and duos, but after concluding that they could not complete the process in less than three years, they gave up the attempt in 1984. Mel Litoff said, "Unfortunately, the bureaucracy of New York City does not see itself in a supportive role to help well-meaning people who want to comply, to make it possible to do it. The standards are contradictory. It's a miracle that anyone has been able to comply with the requirements in New York. It's *very* costly"[6]

For many clubs, the licensing route was all but out of the question. They either were not in a proper zone for cabarets, or they had no extra money to go through the licensing process; the City's "only the strong survive" licensing policy made it next to impossible for them to become licensed. The proprietor of the Angry Squire was quoted, "I have commercial zoning, and I'll pay my annual whatever for a . . . permit. But it's hard to put thirty grand into this small place. Why should I have to have the same license as a big dance hall with thousands of teenagers? This is a listening-only club with seventy seats; you can fit a hundred people in if they hold their breath."[7]

Most of the clubs were small, and in the exploding real estate market, they were increasingly marginal. Art D'Lugoff, who had contrived to keep the Village Gate going for nearly thirty years, said, "The main problem is real estate. . . . The developers have upped the price of commercial as well as residential leases and, without some mechanism to keep them down, there's almost no way to keep a new club afloat." As Stuart Troup of *Newsday* remarked, in a piece collecting the complaints of club owners, "jazz is an economically marginal activity." He quoted some bleak advice from Mel Litoff: "Those who are in it and are talented at what they do, can eke out a basic profit from it. . . . There is no big money in it. . . . It takes enormous effort, in terms of knowledge of the music, management skills and knowledge of running a club, to keep it going."[8]

Under these circumstances, unlicensed clubs tried to tailor their music to the "incidental musical entertainment" exception. The Burgundy Cafe, as we have seen, stopped using saxophones and began to emphasize the piano and to hire singers. At Gregory's, Warren Chiasson stopped playing vibraphone and switched to piano in the Chuck Wayne trio on Tuesday nights. Discovery, in 1985 a new place at Broome and Mercer Streets in Soho, took the ingenious approach of offering a trio of Reggie Workman on bass, Stanley Cowell on Piano and violinist Ali Akbar.[9]

Horn players went around looking for work. Bob Belden, a young saxophonist fresh from the big bands, tried to play his demonstration tape at the West End Bar but the management told him they could not hire sax players. Belden heard the same story at 55 Christopher Street, a small place in Greenwich Village.[10]

Some clubs bucked the law, operated illegally and prayed that they would not get summonses; those who got away with it had to keep a low profile. The unlicensed places that complied with the law by hiring small groups often did not draw well. For the most part, the trios or smaller groups were not natural to the idiom. With the exception of the development of the bass–piano duo, jazz required larger groups and people expected drums and saxophones. And all this was occurring in a real estate market with rising rents. The result was that the musicians were paid as badly as they had ever been; they would sometimes work an entire evening for forty or fifty dollars, or for nothing at all except what could be collected from the patrons by passing a hat.

The union felt unable to alleviate the situation by directly intervening to bargain with the clubs. Many clubs were economically fragile and many musicians did not want to create a confrontation with them because they needed the clubs, if only as places where they might get a hearing in New York. And in any case, the independent contractor and permanent replacement rules in the labor laws made it difficult to bargain effectively with the clubs on behalf of the musicians.

And even so clubs were constantly going out of business, or abandoning a music policy because it was too much of a hassle. The Burgundy closed, to name just the smallest of several, as did Discovery in Soho. The combination of rising rents, the licensing system and the always-marginal popularity of jazz was strangling music clubs in New York.

It was at the beginning of the period of renewed enforcement, in 1983, that the Glasel administration came into office at Local 802, had its meeting with the jazz musicians, and resolved to attack the cabaret ordinance. The union leaders did not know that in 1955 Local 802 had sponsored the very exception for "incidental musical entertainment" that they were now attacking. By the time the provision had made its way into the licensing ordinance in 1961, its origins were forgotten.

In the mid 1980s, we would all have been astounded to learn what John Glasel's predecessor of 1955 had intended. We would have been amazed to learn that a principal purpose of the strings-and-keyboards exception had been to encourage mellifluous behind-the-potted-palms trios, because such music had almost passed from the restaurant scene in the intervening twenty-odd years; it was so far gone that its reappearance on one occasion in the eighties made the *New York Times*.[11] Instead, the exception had served to distort the music that was actually being played in restaurants. The purpose announced in 1955 of preventing the congregation of "undesirable elements" would have confirmed our worst suspicions about the racism and more general discrimination that lay behind the exception. Although the City would not admit to such a purpose in the eighties, the policy was not quite abandoned, as we were to discover in the course of our litigation.

THE CITY COUNCIL

The union was able to enlist the aid of Ruth Messinger in drafting and introducing a local law to change the "incidental musical entertainment" exception. As one of the few members of the City Council who brought a left perspective to city politics, Messinger was concerned for the musicians' livelihood. She recalls:

> Music was not my field of expertise, although I had done something about it before—to try to prevent the City from losing one of its jazz radio stations. What led up to this was that one of the areas in which I had learned a lot was the matter of small business. As a result, I was always doing things to emphasize that the people who do the small, the less lucrative things, the retail things, are critical to the city. Musicians and Off-Broadway theater, for example, are essential. When they think about business in the city, the City thinks of the garment industry, or the airlines. But smaller businesses matter just as much. Hundreds of thousands of people make their living that way.
>
> So it was part of a whole piece for me: that the City

should give less help to bigger business and more to smaller business.

Another thing is, it is interesting to find a piece of City law that is totally irrational. The clause that said only three people could play certain kinds of instruments was—dumb. It is always a pleasure to try to change that kind of thing.

As part of her "whole piece," Messinger had also introduced a bill intended to limit commercial rents for small businesses by providing for binding arbitration of rent increases. If this bill had passed, it might have helped to stabilize the clubs financially. Unfortunately, this was one proposed measure that earned her the enmity of the Koch administration and never passed.

The union leadership thought that getting a complete change in the regulation of music, including the limitation on the number of instruments, would be "a piece of cake," in Judy West's words.[13] But knowing they were in for a fight, Messinger warned them that they were going to have to start small, with a change in the discrimination against horns and percussion. Her bill simply defined "incidental musical entertainment" to be that produced by mechanical devices or three live musicians; in other words, it eliminated the discrimination without changing the three-musician rule.

Messinger's caution about the City Council proved to be well-founded. The bill went to the Committee on Consumer Affairs, chaired by Carol Greitzer from Greenwich Village. Greitzer, like Mayor Koch himself, was one of the politicians who had gone through the fights against entertainment in the Village in the sixties and seventies. Perhaps that experience made Greitzer say that if the bill were passed, "you could have 14,000 restaurants having jazz combos, and many of them are in residential zones."[14] Mistrusting any change in the cabaret laws, she was not about to give in on percussion and horns. She began by raising the issue of noise.

Although one announced purpose of the melange of instru-

ments in the 1955 definition of incidental musical entertainment
had been to minimize noise, it was clear to the union in the
eighties that the law completely failed to serve that purpose.
On the one hand, the definition was an outright expression of
prejudice: the musicians knew that an able musician can play
any instrument softly. On the other hand, the law was completely out of date; under contemporary conditions of electronic
amplification, a stringed instrument such as a guitar can be
played at deafening volume. Nevertheless, in the effort to get
the discrimination eliminated, Glasel and Local 802 recruited
expert advice on noise levels to help draft a bill limiting the
decibel level of noise legally audible outside an establishment
with amplified music.[15] Glasel hoped the Messinger bill and the
noise bill would be passed as a package.

In June, 1985, the Consumer Affairs Committee held a hearing on the Messinger bill to eliminate the discrimination in
instruments, at which a seven-piece union band played Duke
Ellington's "Satin Doll," once very loudly and then very softly.
It seemed to me that they were not very well received. One
committee member, who claimed to know something about
popular music, sneered "Nobody plays music that low."[16] Although many neighborhood people testified about noisy places
near them, they were all, as far as I could tell, complaining
about raucous bars or discotheques. No one had a complaint
specifically about live music, much less about a trio, with or
without percussion. Wearing my law-professor hat, I testified
for the bill. In the course of my testimony, I suggested, based
on a few cases, that the existing discrimination was unconstitutional. Ms. Greitzer asked me, "Thinking of bringing a lawsuit,
professor?" She was tempting me; up to that point, I had not
thought about it seriously.

The union's strategy of combining a bill to limit noise with
the bill ending the discrimination against horns and percussion
did not work. The two bills were assigned to different commit-
tees, and the noise bill was reported out and passed, while the
cabaret reform was bottled up.

At the end of the year, John Glasel went diplomatically to the signing of the noise-limitation ordinance,[17] although it could not have been a very happy occasion. As it turned out, however, the law was a strategic victory, clearing the way for a much neater set of legal arguments in the later suit against the cabaret ordinance.

I began to be persuaded that the Messinger amendment to the cabaret laws, however small its intended effect, was not going to be passed. The head of the committee opposed the bill, and there was no countervailing political force that could shake it loose from the committee. We could not swing the Koch administration around to our point of view. Repeatedly at hearings we heard from club owners and musicians that the licensing, combined with the real estate market, was killing the clubs and consequently the music. Nevertheless I think the city administration as well as many of the council members did not believe the picture painted at the hearings. Sympathy for club owners never runs very high; and in a hustling, rich town like New York it is just very difficult to convince people that important cultural resources may be offered in bars and restaurants that are the entertainment equivalents of Mom-and-Pop stores. At some level, then, many of the City's politicians did not care about the music or think that it was important. They would not take even the smallest political risk of annoying constituents or other politicians to amend the ordinance. What we needed to change their minds was not better arguments, but power. We did not have it.

At this point, I began to realize that we were making the same mistake that the union had made in 1955 and the City Council had made in the coffeehouse licensing of 1961: We were failing to coordinate zoning with the licensing ordinance. The Messinger bill was drafted to change the licensing ordinances, but not the Zoning Resolution, which restricted the neighborhoods where groups larger than a trio of strings and keyboards could play; the zoning change had been the union's "reform" of 1955. We had yet to understand why the City clung to its old zoning restrictions. And we were even farther from understanding how difficult it would be to change them.

ZONING POLICY

The rhetoric justifying the "incidental musical entertainment" exception in the Zoning Resolution had shifted a little since 1955. Noise was no longer mentioned as a rationale; technology had overtaken it. But the policy in favor of polite background music remained essentially unchanged, even though the purpose of controlling "wild strangers" was no longer so frankly expressed. During the course of the litigation, the Chief Engineer of the Department of City Planning was to say:

> . . . In order to establish a consistent and objective standard for this restriction, a limit was placed on the number of musicians providing such entertainment (three) and the types of instruments played (piano, organ, accordion and other stringed instruments) [*sic*]. The Board of Estimate along with the City Planning Commission, determined that this would result in developing establishments most consistent with the rationale behind Use Group 6, i.e. providing local service establishments to fill local residential needs. The distinction would thus permit and encourage neighborhood restaurants or bars to provide background music. The instruments chosen were and are closely associated with establishments, such as piano bars and restaurants with roving violins, which the drafters of the Resolution determined were appropriate for residential neighborhoods.
>
> If the number of musicians were left undetermined or if brass or percussion instruments were permitted in a Use Group 6 establishment, the establishment might no longer be providing "incidental" music; instead entertainment could become the major attraction, thus resulting in larger regional patronage. If that were the case

. . . then it may be that congestion from pedestrian and
automotive traffic could result in a diminution of the
quality of life in that area.[18]

The Zoning Resolution permitted bars and restaurants to
apply for a cabaret license in districts designated for major commercial centers, "high-bulk commercial" centers (usually im-
plying big buildings), amusement parks, and mixed commercial-industrial districts, as well as in manufacturing districts,
which generally have few residences of any kind.[19] It is for this
reason that in recent years we are sometimes treated to the
eerie sight of limousines pulling up in the dead of night to a
discotheque hidden on an industrial street that is otherwise totally deserted; that is the sort of neighborhood in which it is least
difficult to get a cabaret license.

One of the commercial districts, C5, called the "gilt-edged"
district, is "intended primarily for high-quality retail uses," such
as those found on Fifth Avenue in Midtown. Entertainment was
not supposed to be permitted there at all, except in large hotels.
The Guardian Life Company, located on Park Avenue South at
17th Street, in a C5 district, threatened suit in 1967 when the
City granted a zoning variance for the nearby restaurant, Max's
Kansas City, to open a nightclub. Guardian Life's opposition
might seem odd at first, since the block had no residences and
was otherwise deserted at night. The point, it is clear, was to
maintain the tone of a gilt-edged commercial neighborhood, in
which such pursuits as dancing and music were not permitted
outside the staid confines of a hotel.[20]

Entertainment was also not permitted in a C1, or local retail
district, of the sort that the Chief Engineer was describing. "Use
Group 6," New York zoning jargon for the commercial uses
permitted in a C1 district, encompassed local services like gro-
cery stores and restaurants, such as are found along Upper
Broadway in Manhattan. Thus the characterization of the neighborhoods involved in the Chief Engineer's statement as "residential" was slightly misleading; in purely residential districts, the

issue of entertainment would never come up, because commercial establishments such as bars and restaurants are not permitted. The nightmare of a hot band blaring out on a tree-lined street in Queens, cited from time to time in debates at the City Council, could not come to pass; such streets are not found in commercial districts.

The overall thrust of the zoning policy concerning live music was tolerably clear: to interdict any music that might attract a listening audience in restaurants or bars in local neighborhoods or gilt-edged retail districts. The entire slant of the Zoning Resolution thus ran against the existence of small music clubs in local neighborhoods. The justifications concealed a tangle of prejudices and assumptions.

One such assumption is that local neighborhoods are made more livable and safe if they are quiet and nearly deserted. This model centers on the nuclear family, taking as its aim the preservation of privacy, tolerating the minimum commercial development necessary to the conduct of family life. The ideal is that of a controlled world, the denizens of which can have as much or as little contact with others as they want to. A corollary is that contact with strangers from outside the community is something to be avoided, something that interferes with the controlled environment.

Some upper-middle class suburbs approach this ideal. They have little or no public space at all, and all municipal endeavors are directed at protecting private families and residents from local as well as outside intrusion. Such minimal public social intervention as goes on between residents is generally not conducted by direct contact and negotiation, but through complaints to officials such as the police.[21]

It would be a mistake, however, to identify this ideal exclusively with suburbs; many of them, after all, are intensely social and community-minded.[22] The same ideal, moreover, has appeared repeatedly in urban planning. In her famous diatribe, *The Death and Life of Great American Cities,* Jane Jacobs put her finger on a thread running through the history of planning: that in the dream of a better city, a City Beautiful, there was the image of a controlled environment.[23] Using a local neighborhood, rather than a city-wide perspective, we might call this the controlled community ideal.

City zoning policy and planning is often infused with this ideal. William H. Whyte, who has long crusaded for the proposition that people, at least people in cities, like to crowd together much better than they like to be alone, has recently written:

> Too much empty space and too few people—this finally emerges as the problem of the center in more cities than not. It had been the problem for a long time, but the lag in recognizing it as such was lamentably long. . . .
>
> It is sad to see how many cities have this emptiness at their core. It is sadder still to see how many are adopting exactly the approaches that will make matters worse. Most of their programs have as a stated purpose "relief from pedestrian congestion." There is no pedestrian congestion. What they need is pedestrian congestion.
>
> . . . the approaches that work best are those which meet the city on its own gritty terms; which raise the density, rather than lower it; which concentrate, tightening up the fabric, and get the pedestrian back on the street.[24]

The Project for Public Spaces, a consulting firm for urban planning in New York, is dedicated to putting similar ideas into practice. The director of this Project, Fred Kent, uses the concept "retail" to describe the interplay between public space and private interests. Retail is the nexus where trade is conducted on a face-to-face basis, and where personal communication, including gossip, takes place. In a city, this interplay tends to be diverse, vital and messy; in a retail district there are crowds of people who are, in one way or another, concerned with what is going on. A shopping mall next to a highway, so often neat, clean, and empty, is the antithesis of retail.[25]

Neat and clean spaces are empty because they are not interesting; on the contrary, the very diversity of life on the city street tends to pull people into it. A corollary to this would be that empty spaces are not safe, at least outside an upper-middle class suburb in which the presence of strangers can be effectively monitored and controlled. In cities, empty streets are often dangerous. The presence of a constant flow of pedestrians tends to make the streets safe, and to make people aware of the fact that they are safe, so that they will venture out into the city.[26]

The conflict of values between this urban diversity ideal and the controlled community ideal has been constant in New York City in the recent past. When the present form of the Zoning Resolution was introduced in 1961, it provided for incentives to builders to provide public spaces. The "plaza bonus," which permitted developers to increase the size of a building in return for providing a public plaza, was expected to produce more amenities for those on the street. In fact, as critics point out, the "open spaces provided in return, far from offering the 'tower in the park' ideal, have been, in many instances, bleak and uninviting, and viewed by the communities they were meant to benefit as a poor trade-off. . . ."[27] A large part of the reason, as William H. Whyte has remarked, is that the "amenities" were not usually linked to the life of the City; not having traffic in them, they did not attract traffic. They did not have retail uses, and thus people shunned them. It seems likely that many developers did not really want the public to use the spaces, because that would have made them less neat and controllable; in fact, some of the spaces came to seem forbidding and dangerous, especially at night. While many of the abuses of the system of "incentive zoning" have been improved in recent years, the City has always shown itself only fumblingly and intermittently interested in diverse and democratic retail exchanges.[28]

At a much less grand level, the Lindsay administration tried in the sixties to encourage sidewalk cafes, which were all but nonexistent at that time, in the effort to increase street life. They permitted street entertainers, who had formerly been harassed by the police, as well as performers in the parks. Sidewalk cafes and street entertainment caught on and developed apace; in the late seventies, the Koch administration found that there were two hundred unlicensed sidewalk cafes, and began trying to enforce a licensing policy for them.[29]

Fred Kent points out that New York is more hospitable to diverse and entertaining street uses than most American cities, which often forbid sidewalk cafes, the display of fruits and vegetables in open markets, and cooking on peddler's carts. Significantly, they do it pursuant to the health code, in the name of sanitation. Once again: neat, clean—and empty.[30]

Richard Sennett has found a general tendency in the administration of modern cities to encourage a withdrawal from public spaces into the family, and subtly to identify public life as dirty or immoral.[31] Evening gathering places, such as cafes, bars and restaurants, which can be retail uses, encouraging people to get out in the streets and circulate at night, are under constant pressure in this process. Indeed, American planning literature, even when it is most supportive of the urban diversity ideal, has almost nothing to say about the social function of such public gathering places for adults. Ray Oldenburg, in his canvas of what he calls the "third places" of informal public life, puts it more strongly: "American planners and developers have shown a great disdain for those earlier arrangements in which there was life beyond home and work."[32] Richard Sennett remarks, "American zoning has been very puritanical about this. Americans think that one's place is in the home."[33]

With virtually nothing in American zoning policy to make a special place for entertainment uses, then, the Lindsay administration's reaction was ambivalent. After abolishing the most notorious abuse—the cabaret cards system—the administration seemed unable to decide what to do about the licensing of clubs. They vacillated about the coffeehouses that had entertainment, alternately wanting to let them flourish or to close them down, depending on local pressure. The coffeehouse licensing law passed in 1961, which scarcely differed from the cabaret licensing system, was hardly used, and was ultimately abandoned. In

1971, Lindsay signed a bill amending the "incidental musical entertainment" exception to permit bars and restaurants without cabaret licenses to have a singer accompanied by a piano or a string instrument; it was dubbed "the folk-singer exception." Apart from that, the rule persisted in limiting live music to a trio consisting of keyboards and strings.[34] The Koch administration, as shown in the last chapter, at first enforced the cabaret laws flexibly, and then rigidly.

In his opinion that brass and percussion were not appropriate in a local commercial district, the City Planning Department's Chief Engineer drew heavily on the ideal of the controlled community; he made an assumption that the "quality of life" in a local neighborhood is better if strangers are not coming into it, walking its streets and going into bars in the evening. Under the surface, the exclusion of strangers turns out to be what the longing for clean and sanitized neighborhoods is almost always about. As William H. Whyte remarked, "The old phrase, 'there goes the neighborhood' was just an excuse to keep out people of a lower type. But the idea that if you keep a neighborhood insulated, it will be just ducky, does not work. If you wall off the neighborhood, you get a dead neighborhood. . . . People knock themselves out to keep out bad people—and usually don't succeed."[35]

The engineer's statement, primarily through what it did not say, betrayed a prejudice about the sort of people who are attracted to music clubs. The statement did not mention the fact that restaurants or popular bars were freely permitted in local retail districts, with no attempt to restrict those uses to local people. As I wrote during the course of the litigation, ". . . it seems rather likely that restaurants that serve the fashionable cuisine of the moment, whether it be the sashimi of Japan or the blackened redfish of the cajun country, attract crowds from outside the neighborhood. The city does not insist that a restaurant serve, say, meat loaf or chicken *a la king* in order to discourage those from outside the neighborhood from queuing up at the restaurant."[36] But the city did insist that the restaurant serve only "background music." The conclusion was almost inescapable that strangers who were attracted to a local neighborhood by its food were more desirable than those who were attracted by its music. The "wild strangers" and "degenerates," were, it seems, alive and well in the imagination of city officials—and ready to push in and listen to hot music. It was the old apprehension about the "jazz crowd," rooted in racism and fear of the hip and oppositional.

The engineer's statement betrayed a second, connected prejudice: that there is no such thing as a neighborhood jazz club, in which bands without famous musicians will simply play, using horns and drums, for the drinkers or diners who walk into the joint. It envisioned nothing but a big-time nightclub that attracts people from all over—people, moreover, whom one would just as soon not have in the neighborhood.

An expert land-use lawyer remarked to me that the Zoning Resolution, having been adopted in 1961, necessarily embodied social ideas about land use from the forties and fifties. The Chief Engineer's examples of background music—piano bars and restaurants with roving violins—seemed to emanate from that era, or even earlier, though he was speaking in 1986, and the notions about music clubs and their patrons that he attributed to the Zoning Resolution were equally antiquated. By the time the Chief Engineer made his affidavit, the cabaret laws were increasingly irrelevant to clubs that offered only live music. During the course of the litigation, David Sheldon at Local 802 organized a group of volunteers, employees as well as musicians who presumably had free time on account of the cabaret laws, to survey the ninety-four licensees named by the Department of Consumer Affairs as located in Manhattan in the spring of 1986. They found that only forty made use of the license, in the sense that they sometimes offered more music—jazz or any other kind—than they could have offered without it; among the others were discos, strip-joints without live music, and nonexistent nightspots—those which had gone out of business. On the other hand, in 1984, Sheldon, curious to know how many bars and restaurants actually had live music, had ". . . canvassed an entire area . . . from Avenue A to the Hudson River, and from Four-teenth Street to Chambers Street [in Manhattan], looking for places that offered some live music." He went on to say, "I found approximately one hundred such places. I was not aware at that time which clubs have cabaret licenses, but I have no doubt that the overwhelming majority of the places I visited did not have licenses."[37]

Many places that had music were too small, too poor or did not attach enough importance to music to apply for a cabaret license. The licensing system made it difficult to have music on a casual, neighborhood basis, or as an experiment, except for a piano or background music. There were hole-in-the-wall places that risked larger, more complete jazz groups, like Augie's, a tiny bar on Broadway near 106th Street. Such places can become important, because very good, unknown musicians may play, and others may come in to jam, as they have done at Augie's in recent years.

On the other hand, the purely local neighborhood businesses, of which the Chief Engineer spoke so confidently, found it increasingly difficult to continue under prevailing real estate conditions. There were a thousand anecdotes about extraordinary jumps in rent; Barry Harris closed his Jazz Cultural Theater on Eighth Avenue in 1987 when the landlord increased the rent from $3000 to $5000 a month, although Harris had a great many other problems as well, including the lack of a cabaret license. The Mayor's Small Retail Business Study Commission of 1986, which rejected proposals for rent regulation, nevertheless found that a large percentage of local merchants perceived rent as their most serious problem. Citywide, they reported an increase in rents of 35 per cent over the two years 1983 to '85, but those whose leases had expired in that period reported an increase of 66 per cent. The problem affected every type of local business— dry cleaners, food stores, and drug stores, for example, as well as restaurants. If such establishments could appeal to outsiders, to draw trade from outside the neighborhood, they did so. The

Commission found that consumers were least likely to patronize neighborhood restaurants; that is to say, they would travel to dine out but not to buy shampoo or have a suit cleaned.[38] Thus restaurants were among the very few small retail business that could draw on a regional or city-wide trade for survival, especially in high-rent district in Manhattan. There is a grain of truth, then, in the Chief Engineer's idea that clubs will encourage a regional trade; but it is true because it is essential to their survival, and it is characteristic of bars and restaurants generally.

In the eighties, the viability of purely local retail uses was constantly in doubt, and the ideal of a controlled community was also increasingly subject to question. The idea that it is useful for a city to get people out into its streets, especially at night, in the interests of safety as well as prosperity, was becoming familiar to city officials. The result was policy confusion. In 1985, when discos in Manhattan's East Village were being forced out of business, in part because they could not get licenses, a City official said, "We would look positively on a club that brings people onto the street." And then he added, ". . . But the law is the law."[39]

BARRIERS TO CHANGE IN ZONING POLICY

The Zoning Resolution was increasingly antiquated, largely because it had become so difficult to amend in accord with the changing times. In 1955, when the musicians union had first sought to put the definition of "incidental musical entertainment" in the Zoning Resolution, the mayor, acting with the Board of Estimate, had the power to revise the definition if they chose. By the 1980s that was no longer the case. Changing the Zoning Resolution, which used a definition of "incidental musical entertainment" for land-use purposes, was actually more difficult than the legislative process of changing the city ordinances, which used a similar definition for licensing purposes.

Decisions on land-use planning by the City Planning Commission and the Board of Estimate had provoked a rising tide of community protest during the sixties and seventies. The "urban renewal" model of that period, under which the City might plan, clear and rebuild as it saw fit, was being increasingly rejected. The *New York Times* summed it up in 1975:

> Mention almost any capital project being built by the city. . . . In each instance community groups contend the city tried to run roughshod over community interests and construct developments without informing them fully of their proposals. In each instance, once vocal community opposition mobilized, the project was either modified or shelved.[40]

This public sentiment was part of a general move toward decentralization. The state legislature appointed a committee in 1975 to "write a [City] Charter that would create a genuine citizen participation in local city government."[41] Professional planners were beginning to agree; reporting on a neighborhood conservation conference in 1975, the *New York Times* noted "general agreement on the direction that urban renewal should take—it is towards gradual, incremental renewal, with a strong emphasis on conservation of existing resources, and the independent identity of neighborhoods."[42] The City Planning Commission had already begun to seek the opinion of local community planning groups about proposed projects; the difficulty was that the Commission often did not have any clear standard for determining who spoke for the community. In a very modest decentralization measure, the amended Charter formalized the role of local and borough-wide community boards, with members to be chosen by the Borough President, half of them from nominees of the City Council.[43]

The Community Boards are institutions apparently peculiar to New York City. Almost all proposals for land-use changes must be submitted to them, including changes in the zoning classification of a district (for example from residential to commercial) as well as special permits for uses approved by the

City Planning Commission, such as large building projects. The procedures are collectively called the Uniform Land Use Review Procedures ("ULURP"). For changes in the text of the Zoning Resolution, such as the definition of "incidental musical entertainment," a slightly less demanding procedure is used, which still involves submission to the boards.[44]

Although the boards are not democratically chosen, and have no power to veto a proposal that the City Planning Commission is determined to accept, they have nevertheless made a considerable difference to the planning and zoning process. The Community Boards are required to hold public hearings, at which some local people have been very active in trying to persuade the board of their point of view. Disapproval by a Community Board might lead to a reconsideration of a proposal by the City Planning Commission, or cast doubt on whether the Board of Estimate would approve it. Thus, a proposed change in the definition of "incidental musical entertainment" to allow horns and percussion in bars and restaurants could lead to unpredictable results, depending on how the community boards reacted.

The state Environmental Quality Review Act added still another layer of review that had to be obtained before a change in the Zoning Resolution could be approved. The City Planning Commission was obligated to make a statement about the effect of a proposal on the environment; of course, the Commission could say that a proposal would have no impact (a "negative declaration"), but even so it would have to give the matter study.[45]

The law afforded no way for anyone outside the City Planning Commission to propose a change in the language of the Zoning Resolution; the City Charter had an elaborate system of review by Community Boards, but no way to initiate a proposal. The only way to change the language, then, would be to persuade the City government to do it. But I could not picture the administration wanting to slog through the Community Boards and the environmental review procedures to change the definition of "incidental musical entertainment" in the Zoning Resolution unless someone in the government, preferably at the City Planning Commission, cared a great deal about the issue. I was pretty sure that no one did.

OUT OF THE LABYRINTH

And so we were back to the beginning. The bill to allow horns and percussion was not going to be passed, and if it were passed, Messinger's bill was not going to do the job. Such a regulation was not going to get rid of the three-musician rule. It was not even going to get rid of the discrimination in instruments in a clear-cut way, because it could not change the Zoning Resolution.

All these institutional realities should have led us to reflect on how the law and our perception of practical politics shaped our expectations, our notions of what was political "success." The union lobbied for months and expended a lot of energy in trying to get the Messinger bill passed. If the bill had been passed, it might have worked at least for trios; city agencies might have overlooked the discrepancy with the Zoning Resolution and allowed trios to include horns and percussion. That would have been seen as "success," because at that point we could not focus on trying to revise the cabaret laws to get the clubs with music but no dancing put in a different category—simply to allow bars and restaurants to have such music as they chose, within the confines of the noise code. In retrospect, that was not much to ask; so little, in fact, that if trios had been freely allowed, it is certain that rank and file musicians would have begun another cycle, taking another unforeseeable number of years, to get rid of the three-musician limitation. But that process would have been slowed by the fact that the union had won a recent "victory" in getting rid of the discrimination against horns and percussion.

For better or worse, then, we were confronted at the beginning of 1986 with a situation in which we did not have that small victory defined by a change to an exception in a city ordinance. We could not make any change by political—in the sense of legislative or administrative—means. Not even the tiniest change in the definition of "incidental musical entertainment" was possible for us because the decision-making process was so diffused. Curiously, this resulted in a centralization of power in the mayor's office as the only place that had the clout to coordinate all the fragmentary sources of power.

There was another possibility, one that might cut through the dispersion of the decision process, get all relevant officials to pay attention at once, and achieve a result that would change the licensing ordinance and the zoning provision at the same time. That was a lawsuit.

In my experience lawsuits, at least about public-law issues like the cabaret laws, were almost never fully successful. They seldom won in court, and even when they won, they often failed to bring about the expected results. But lawsuits could change the agenda in unpredictable ways. A decent case—one rooted in arguments that are viable, even if debatable—was an assertion of power. As such the case and publicity around it organized people, and galvanized other people to react, possibly to change or compromise. Public-law litigation was, as it ought to be, a device of last resort.

CHAPTER 6

THE CAMPAIGN TO CHANGE THE LAW: FREE EXPRESSION

BEGINNING THE CASE

From the days of the Lea and Taft-Hartley Acts during Petrillo's presidency of the musicians' union, the union's experience with the law had been a bruising one. In 1983, when the Glasel administration came into office at Local 802, the union had just lost a major "independent contractor" case that the members thought they ought to have won.[1] And, since even their successful cases were painfully protracted, it took a lot of frustration to get the union to repair to the courts. In a press release announcing our case against the cabaret laws John Glasel quoted the old line, "I'm fed up, and I'm not going to take it anymore!"[2] It was not until Glasel and other union officials finally were persuaded that the Messinger bill was not going to be reported out of committee, much less passed, that we began to work seriously on a lawsuit.

The union held another general meeting, on folding chairs in its big hall, to present the idea of the case. Several members, including Warren Chiasson, pressed for an attack on the three-musician limitation; a trio, they said, was just not what their music was about. Although he had always favored such a change, John Glasel was reluctant at first to go that far, probably because he had just emerged from the City Council fight, which was limited to the discrimination against horns and percussion. As Glasel pointed out, eliminating the limit on the number of musicians would completely destroy the distinction between licensed and unlicensed clubs, at least in cases where music alone was being presented. He was not so much opposed to that result, as convinced that the courts would not adopt it. I was not quite so sure. History had presented us with a sharp distinction between places that had social dancing and those that had only live music for listening. The two had been separated socially since the fifties, when the jazz fans walked past Leon and Eddie's on 52nd Street as if it did not exist; the separation had become more radical with the appearance of the discotheques, which drew large crowds but rarely used live music at all. We all agreed that throwing them together under one licensing scheme no longer made any sense, if it ever had. The problem was to translate "no longer makes any sense" into a cogent legal argument.

In the end, the rank and file put us all in a position where we had to make the broader claim to keep our credibility. If the individual musician plaintiffs wanted me to include the claim, I was obligated to include it. And so the union joined the lawsuit to reject the three-musician limitation as well as the discrimination against horns and percussion.

I believe that everyone thought the suit was a desperate last-ditch effort in any case. Certainly nothing in the history of litigation against the cabaret laws encouraged anyone to think otherwise. Every single case against the identity cards had been unsuccessful, and at first glance, this one did not seem any easier.

The dynamics of civil rights litigation, including the pervasive sense of the court's scope of discretion, had changed radically in the years after those cases. The unsuccessful case brought by Nina Simone and others had been decided in 1961, the very year that the U.S. Supreme Court had reinterpreted the old civil rights statutes to expand the federal courts' powers.[3] The Court had ruled that plaintiffs did not have to exhaust their remedies in the states, including the state courts, before they could seek redress for violations of constitutional rights in the federal courts. The notion that federal courts were authorized to take charge of a case and prevent the states from violating rights, combined with a growing "public law" consciousness among the judges during the sixties and seventies, had led to a steady growth of civil rights litigation in the intervening twenty-five years.[4] Although the Supreme Court tried to curtail the federal courts from really reaching down into state institutions and reshaping them, the genie had not been put back in the bottle. The spirit of federal litigation had been changed by the judges' experience of deciding cases to redress unconstitutional acts by state officials. When they were confronted with an attack on a city ordinance, or a set of local practices, the case looked familiar, like the proverbial "federal case." In short, such cases were accepted as within their jurisdiction, not outside it.

I assumed at first without thinking that we would present our case to a federal court. The jurisdiction of the federal courts over such civil rights claims has never been exclusive, however, and after the initial influx into the federal courts in the sixties, many of the cases had been presented to state judges, some of whom, over the course of years, had come to share their federal colleagues' willingness to take action against local political institutions. It might seem, at first glance, that a state judge would be more likely than a federal judge to accept the legitimacy of local law; in 1986, however, this was not necessarily the case. The powers of a federal judge to interfere in a complex local regulatory system were, the Supreme Court had said,[5] somewhat limited. At a more practical level, a state judge was more likely to feel at home with the regulations, to be willing to tinker with them. When I went over a list of the local and state judiciary with other lawyers, after all the years of Nixon and Reagan federal appointments, it seemed to us that we had a slightly better chance in the state court of encountering a judge who would be sympathetic to our First Amendment arguments. As one of the lawyers put it, "When it comes to music in Manhattan, man, get a Manhattan judge!"

While the powers and attitudes of the judiciary were shifting, the law on freedom of expression had been changing at the same time. As the popular arts had become more respectable, the United States Supreme Court had decided that there was no principled way to distinguish between "entertainment" and any other kind of expression, in a case from 1981 that limited the power of municipalities to use zoning to control live entertainment, *Schad v. Borough of Mt. Ephraim.*[6] In that case, a New Jersey suburb had passed a zoning ordinance defining a "commercial zone" in the town so as to permit, for example, restaurants and retail stores, including bookstores, and to forbid any other uses. Interpreted to exclude all "live entertainment" anywhere in Mt. Ephraim, the ordinance was used to punish a bookstore that, for a fee, afforded customers an opportunity to watch a "live nude dancer" through a glass panel. Such a peculiarly antiseptic version of "live entertainment" was perfect for a suburban controlled environment.

And indeed, Mt. Ephraim offered justification for its interpretation, rooted in the "controlled community" tradition, very similar to those the City Planning Department was later to offer for the restrictions on live music in New York. Mt. Ephraim argued, first, that its commercial zoning was designed to cater only to "immediate needs," that is, to supply purely local rather than regional shopping and services, and, second, that forbidding live entertainment was designed "to avoid the problems that may be associated with live entertainment, such as parking, trash, police protection and medical facilities." The U.S. Supreme Court responded to both of these in a similar way, saying that live entertainment could not be functionally distinguished from the uses that were permitted. As to the first, the Court said, "[v]irtually the only item or service that may not be sold in a commercial zone . . . is live entertainment," and as to the second, ". . . it is not immediately apparent . . . that live entertainment poses problems of this nature more significant than those associated with various permitted uses. . . ."[7]

Ordinarily, such zoning classifications would have been

within the power of a municipality; the definitions of local uses, and problems that are alleged to be associated with particular uses, are not usually given close scrutiny by the Court. But this case was different: ". . . when a zoning law infringes upon a protected liberty, it must be narrowly drawn and must further a substantial government interest." The protected liberty at issue in *Schad* was free expression; the key passage for us was:

> . . . the Mount Ephraim ordinance prohibits a wide range of expression that has long been held to be within the protections of the First and Fourteenth Amendments. Entertainment, as well as political and ideological speech, is protected; motion pictures, programs broadcast by radio and television, and live entertainment, such as musical and dramatic works, fall within the First Amendment.[8]

On this central issue of the First Amendment claim we had a strong argument in our case, chiefly based on testimony from David Amram. When I had heard him playing at the Five Spot in the fifties, Amram had been most noted for his work on the French horn, although he also frequently played piano as well as other instruments. In the intervening nearly thirty years, he had become a noted classical composer and conductor. He had composed concertos, sonatas, a string quartet and quantities of incidental music for the New York Shakespeare Festival, as well as two operas. During all those years, he continued to play jazz, saying, "I find that the give and take among the musicians and between the musicians and the audience in such situations is an inspiration to musical creativity." He described the First Amendment interest:

> It is difficult to imagine a more stringent control, short of an absolute prohibition, on the expression of music than the one created by the New York City laws. One effect is basic. The emotional impression that the work of a composer, an individual player or a group of players

makes, depends upon what instruments are used. The same notes, when played on a saxophone or a guitar, convey a very different effect. For example, some of the compositions of J.S Bach, notably the *Musical Offering* and the *Art of the Fugue*, are not scored for designated instruments. When played by varying combinations of instruments, for example, entirely by strings and keyboards, or by wind instruments, or a combination of all of them, these pieces have a different emotional impact. The variety in impression results not only from the timbres of the instruments, but also from a difference in voicing; a musician expresses himself or herself differently, plays the music differently, on different instruments.

These effects are even more important in the case of jazz. Improvised music is particularly idiosyncratic and expressive of the relation between the musician and the instrument. Jazz musicians often utter expressions on particular instruments that cannot be reproduced on other instruments. Restricting the instruments which can be used thus especially restricts expression in jazz music. In acoustical jazz and folk music, it would be hard to imagine this century's output without such practitioners as Louis Armstrong (trumpet), Bix Beiderbecke (trumpet), Gene Krupa (drums), Lester Young (tenor saxophone), Coleman Hawkins (tenor saxophone), Charlie Parker (alto saxophone), Benny Goodman (clarinet), and thousands of others who play wind, brass and percussion instruments.

It would be difficult to imagine compositions, from J.S. Bach to the present, that include wind, brass and percussion, having been written without those instruments. Much of the music, including chamber music, written by Bach, Mozart, Brahms, and Haydn, up through music by George Gershwin, Leonard Bernstein and myself, would have to be totally rewritten or discarded. The history of jazz, folk and Latin American music would have to be rewritten. Wind and percussion instruments are such an integral part of nearly every musical culture including my own, that it is difficult for me as a composer to picture what it would be like to be restricted to creating only for strings and keyboards. It would be like trying to play baseball without the use of outfielders and a catcher.

At the close of his affidavit, he described his own experience with the restriction:

I recently completed a musically exciting and rewarding week playing at Bradley's, an establishment located at 70 University Place . . . Most of the evening, I played the piano. After numerous requests to play at least one melody or do a small amount of improvising using the French horn and various flutes, I obliged on two or three occasions so as not to disappoint the patrons or make them feel I was inconsiderate of their desire to hear me do something I do everywhere else in the world. Because I was trying to do something to the best of my ability for people, some of whom had come from as far away as Sweden and Japan, I had a difficult time explaining to them that I could only play for a minute out of each hour set on instruments they were interested in hearing. I realized, however, that even that minute was illegal.[9]

Nevertheless, although *Schad v. Borough of Mt. Ephraim* created a more friendly atmosphere for First Amendment rights in the vernacular arts, it only began to solve our problems. Unlike the Mt. Ephraim ordinance, the New York City licensing system did not forbid all music or all entertainment; it confined it within certain commercial zones, and limited the sort of music that could be played in the local and gilt-edged commercial zones. The Supreme Court had allowed similar restrictions on free expression through zoning laws, on the theory that they were matters of municipal convenience, so-called "time, place and manner" restrictions. The courts apply four tests in First Amendment cases, requiring the municipality to show that the regulation "(1) is content-neutral, (2) serves a legitimate governmental objective, (3) leaves open ample alternative channels of communication, and (4) is narrowly tailored to serve the governmental objective."[10]

The discriminatory terms of the "incidental musical entertainment" exception helped us to show that there was no legitimate objective, that the ordinance was not narrowly tailored, and that it was not content-neutral.

We were sure that the City could not show that reducing noise was a legitimate objective of the law. Daniel Queen, a noted acoustical engineer who liked to drop in at the Angry Squire, around the corner from his office on Twenty-Third Street, had volunteered to give us expert testimony. He pointed out that under conditions of contemporary electronic amplification, the instruments permitted as "incidental music" could make just as much or more noise as the ones that were forbidden. The exception in the ordinance for music produced by "mechanical devices" made any anti-noise objective still more difficult to justify, because, as Queen said, ". . . it is simpler and cheaper to produce a loud volume of music by mechanical means than it is by using live musicians."[11] The "incidental musical entertainment" exception, furthermore, was not narrowly tailored to control noise. The 1985 ordinance limiting the decibel level of amplified music audible outside the place where it was being played did directly and specifically what the cabaret law seemed to do awkwardly and inefficiently.

Most important, we wanted to show that the exception discriminated on the basis of content through its requirement that any live music in unlicensed clubs be "background music" rather than music played in the way the musicians chose to play it. While we were clear that the City had discriminated against the content of vernacular music, we were not altogether sure that the courts would accept that as "content" in the sense they understand it; the law of free expression has an uneasy relationship to nonverbal expression. About this we wrote:

> In speaking of discrimination against the "content" of expression, the courts have been accustomed to talk in terms of discrimination among "points of view," conceiving of the legal issue primarily as one concerning verbal opinion. Music, of course, does not usually set forth "points of view" or "opinions" in the same sense. The content-discrimination is rather with respect to the style and instrumentation of the music, but it is nevertheless must as surely a discrimination against the special musical ideas which plaintiffs want to express through their instruments, as well as against the range of expression that is available through the sounds, voicings and peculiarities of varied combinations of instruments.[12]

Warren Chiasson was an example. He was required to play piano at Gregory's when he would have much preferred to play the vibraphone. While I was in Gregory's collecting an affidavit from Chuck Wayne in 1986, the guitarist asked if I was going to win the case. "I hope you do," he said, looking over at Chiasson. "Warren is a good piano player. But he is a *great* vibraphonist."

I thought our case was in a stronger position—was presented in a better atmosphere for a liberty argument—because it was brought by musicians, the people whose expression was actually being infringed. All the other cases had involved the clubs rather than musicians, and many had involved dancing. Although technically these had been free expression cases, they were shadowed by the fact that those who brought them were trying to conduct a nightclub business; the powers of the municipality to zone or license businesses loomed larger in those cases. Ours was a case in which the artists themselves were plaintiffs, explaining to the court exactly what was lost to them in expression through the ordinance. It was, in an intangible way, a more sympathetic case.

It did not come about by design. I would not have objected, at first, to including a club as a plaintiff. But the people at Local 802 thought there was too much potential for a conflict if a club was included in the case; the union might end up negotiating a contract or mounting a job action against the place. As we prepared the case, furthermore, I found that some of the club owners were not reliable allies. One of them scoffed at the idea of a lawsuit, saying, "you don't need a lawsuit, you need power." (True, of course, but not helpful). Another owner, having made a decent living employing underpaid musicians for years, refused to give me an affidavit stating that he would like to hire a bigger band, on the grounds that the "city might come back on me." In short, some club owners thought they had something to lose in the case, while the musicians did not.

The musicians themselves, who had become accustomed over years of working with the union to think of the cabaret problem as an issue of jobs—of replacing canned with live music—also began to think of the case as presenting an issue of liberty. Ironically, it became more a liberty than a bread-and-butter case just because the clubs, especially the unlicensed clubs, paid so badly. Warren Chiasson put it well, as I recall: "The point is, if you are a jazz musician, you have to get a hearing in New York to reach the audience and let them know who you are. It isn't the money, because we don't get paid enough to matter in these places."

Having only the art of music to consider presented the court with a clean and pointed constitutional issue concerning content-regulation and legitimate municipal regulatory interests. The music issue automatically separated us from the dance clubs legally, as had been done socially over the course of so many years. This turned out to be fortunate, because shortly after the decision in our case, the U.S. Supreme Court was to decide in a zoning case that there is no substantial First Amendment interest in social dancing, at least in a club,[13] a decision that I found regrettable but not very surprising. The time for constitutional recognition of vernacular music might have arrived, but the time for recognition of the expressive force of vernacular social dancing had not yet come. And other sorts of entertainment, such as dancing as performance, would have presented unpredictable zoning issues.

Nevertheless, ours was a chancy case. There were a number of court decisions about the city's cabaret-licensing system and similar systems, some suggesting in passing that it was constitutionally infirm, and some upholding it, but none, of course, striking it down.[14] The difficulty with our case was that it depended on a combination of malleable concepts, like the judge's estimate of how strong the City's interest in the ordinance was, and also upon matters of taste. If the judge did not care for jazz or some other sort of music that is played in clubs, he was not likely to care whether the ordinance was "content-neutral" or not, or even to grasp how the content issues applied in our case.

Although the cabaret laws had been on the books for decades, they now seemed intolerable to the musicians. We could not wait months for a trial, while musicians were being deprived of chances to play. We filed the case in May of 1986, together with a motion for an expedited hearing through a preliminary injunction. Chuck Wayne submitted an affidavit that Warren Chiasson would be able to play vibraphone the very next week at Gregory's if the motion was granted, and Monica Hughes said that horn players like Mark Morganelli could go to work again immediately at the Burgundy Cafe. The courts had ruled that the deprivation of a First Amendment right was "irreparable injury" for purposes of injunctive relief, so we had the basic elements to win our motion if the court was at all sympathetic to our constitutional claims.[15]

Cases were assigned to judges by lot out of a box at the clerk's office. By the luck of the draw, our case was sent to Acting Justice David Saxe, sitting in a part of the court for cases against the City. Saxe had, almost ten years before, been Director of Enforcement for the chief defendant, the Department of Consumer Affairs. Lawyers I talked to were quite unable to read him at that point; all we knew for sure was that we had taken a risk by bringing the case into state court.

The publicity, at least, could hardly have been more sympathetic. The attitude of the press toward the popular arts had changed in the generation since the demise of the cabaret-identity cards. There were critics and commentators for the major newspapers who made their living writing about jazz, rock, ethnic music, indeed all sorts of music other than the classics. They took the music seriously; it was no longer just part of a "nightclub beat." In April, the *New York Times* had reported on the crackdown on clubs, and published an op-ed piece against the law's restrictions by David Levy, then at the New School. The case was reported favorably, and in June, the *Times* ran an editorial questioning even the three-musician rule.[16]

In the answering papers to the motion, we finally found out what the City thought was the "legitimate governmental objective" of the regulation of music. The City Planning Department's Chief Engineer filed his affidavit, discussed in the last chapter, saying that the purpose was to prevent unlicensed clubs from offering more than background music because "it may be that congestion from pedestrian and automotive traffic could result in a diminution of the quality of life in that area."[17] Nothing more. Noise was out of the case; the testimony of acoustical engineer Daniel Queen and the ordinance limiting amplified music had done their work.

I was somewhat surprised that the City had not advanced fire-safety as one of its objectives, because increased safety requirements for clubs were of recent vintage. A safety argument would have done nothing, however, to explain the zoning restrictions, and very little to explain the licensing system. The Fire Department had the power to enforce the safety regulations against clubs, just as it enforced all the other fire laws, by periodic inspections, summonses and criminal penalties. A complex licensing system, not to speak of zoning, was not essential for fire-law enforcement.

About a month later, Justice Saxe filed his opinion preliminarily enjoining the discrimination against horns and percussion; he refused, however, to enjoin the "incidental musical entertainment" exception as a whole. He accepted the City's argument on this point, saying, ". . . the limit on the number of musicians who can play in these clubs directly furthers the City's interest in managing traffic congestion and preserving the quality and character of the particular neighborhood."[18] Within a very few days, the City Council, at the request of the mayor, suddenly accepted a bill much like the Messinger bill, and made the preliminary relief into a city ordinance.

At first this felt a little like victory. It was an object lesson in how litigation can sometimes be used in place of other sources of power to get a legislative result. But it seemed that way, I believe, just because almost everyone had previously thought that the case was going to fail entirely. But Peter LaRoca Sims and all the other musicians who thought that the limitation on the size of bands was irrational did not think it was much of a victory. They wanted to sweep away the restrictions; the case had raised expectations, and now the musicians wanted the relief we had asked for.

Indeed, the situation for music in the clubs was not improved. In a move reminiscent of the police reaction to criticism of the identity cards in 1960, the crackdown by the Department of Consumer Affairs appeared to intensify during the next year. The agency took action against a new club, the Whippoorwill, at 18 East 18th Street, that was hiring noted musicians and paying them well. The *New York Times* critic John S. Wilson reviewed an engagement there by trumpeter Jack Walrath, who, having written arrangements for a septet, was obliged to rescore them for a trio with drums and an electric bass. Wilson drily commented, "This sometimes results in a rather fuzzy suggestion of an ensemble."[19]

The Eagle Tavern, on West 14th Street near Ninth Avenue, which had for years been a haven for several kinds of vernacular music other than jazz, including Bluegrass, Irish and Scottish music, was reduced to trios. Dan Lynch's, a tiny blues bar on Second Avenue near 14th Street, was forced into the same position. At those places, as well as at several others, the bands tried to circumvent the law by playing musical chairs; if a quartet was playing, one of the musicians stood aside while the other three played. Freddy's Supper Club, a showcase for ballad singers on East 49th Street that *Newsday's* Stuart Troup found very promising, was fined six hundred dollars for using accompaniments that were more than "incidental music." Sutton's, a restaurant on West 145 Street that was struggling to bring more jazz to Harlem, was twice given summonses. Also cited were the Cajun, an excellent restaurant on Eighth Avenue that has New Orleans-style music with its creole food, and Jimmy Walker's, which had Bill and George Simon's Swing Group on Wednesday evenings. All in all, Consumer Affairs issued 110 summonses for unlicensed clubs during the year 1987.[20]

The best-known case was that of Mikell's, which had been open at 97th Street and Amsterdam Avenue for seventeen years without ever hearing that there was such a thing as a cabaret law. In May, 1986, Mike Mikell had paid a fine for violating the law. In February, 1987, police and the Department of Consumer Affairs arrived to padlock the club. Appearing as it did to be a "raid," it hurt business badly even after the padlock was taken off. In addition, the club was fined $4500 and had to use trios. Mike Mikell had booked Art Blakey and the Jazz Messengers, a septet, for the weekend following the raid, and was forced to ask Art Blakey to have the musicians take turns, three at a time. Blakey finally threw down his drumsticks in disgust, exclaiming, "I can't play trio!"[21]

For the first time, the press was taking persistent notice of the effects of cabaret licensing. The summonses and the shift to trios at Whippoorwill, the Angry Squire, the West End, the Eagle Tavern, Dan Lynch's and Mikell's were all reported, often very unfavorably to the city. The *New York Times* music critic Jon Pareles cracked, "Musicians and club patrons . . . say that increased enforcement of the cabaret law has helped turn New York, the world's jazz capital, into Trio City." The *New Yorker* in its "Goings On About Town" listings for April 6, 1987, noted that "Prohibition-age" laws were limiting Mikell's to three musicians; the "Insider's Guide" in *New York* magazine for May 4, took note of the effects of the "incidental musical entertainment" exclusion.[22]

As Stuart Troup of *Newsday* was reporting, clubs were going out of business, partly because jazz was an economically marginal activity, partly because of the three-musician rule. Discovery, the little place in Soho that had tried to comply with the law by hiring a piano, bass and violin trio, dropped its music policy.[23] Meanwhile, enforcement continued to appear rather haphazard. Several places consistently booked bands larger than trios, and never heard a thing from the city, among them Visiones on MacDougal Street, the Knitting Factory on Houston Street, and Teddy's on Berry Street in Brooklyn.[24]

SUMMARY JUDGMENT

As the situation with the musicians, the press, the clubs and the enforcement authorities was coming to a boil, we were trying to get the case ready for trial. My colleague Claudia Angelos at NYU Law School joined the case with students from her law clinic. At the beginning of 1987, we served notices to take the depositions of some city officials by way of pre-trial discovery, chiefly in the effort to find out why they thought a bigger band, of, say, four or five, was going to hurt the quality of life in local commercial neighborhoods.

The City's response was to move for summary judgment— in effect a motion to dismiss before trial based on the entire record in the case, on the ground that there are no triable issues. The motion was in many ways a natural one. In the decision on the preliminary injunction, the judge had appeared wholly to accept the justification for the limitation to three musicians; there was reason to think that he would say that the question was settled, and would dismiss the case. Nevertheless, summary judgment motions are tricky at best, and especially so early in the litigation. The moving party has to lay out his entire case in affidavit form, and show that he would actually be able to prove every factual allegation he needs. The answering party has an only slightly easier task; he can say that he needs pre-trial discovery to prove one or more of his points, but if he has absolutely nothing to show in the way of proof on the point, he is likely to find himself dismissed by the court. In the New York courts, the most risky aspect of the motion is that the court "searches the record," as the expression is, for all the parties, and can grant summary judgment against the moving party if the judge thinks that the other side has proved its case, while the moving party has failed. The court always has the power to take such an action, although it is unusual to do so unless the party opposing the motion asks for it. The only safe way to handle such a motion, on either side, is to prepare affidavits to prove every material point in the case as solidly as you would for trial.

We strengthened and clarified our proof that the regulation failed on all four legs of the justification for a "time, place and manner restriction"—that it discriminated as to content, that adequate alternative channels of communication were insufficient, and that there was no legitimate objective to which the regulation was narrowly tailored.[25]

We showed in detail how the limitation to "background music" by at most a trio created discrimination against the content of most vernacular music. Jack Walrath described how the limitation had ruined the arrangements he had written for the engagement at Whippoorwill in 1986. Jon Pareles of the *New York Times*, producer and critic Michael Cuscuna, as well as John Glasel, all explained that most forms of jazz cannot be played adequately by a trio; Dixieland jazz, for example, was missing from the city in part because it uses at least five and generally six instruments—three horns and three rhythm—to get adequate balance and counterpoint. The proper balance for modern jazz is somewhat more flexible, but is rooted in a basic form of three rhythm and one or more horns. Trumpeter Mark Morganelli described how he had a difficult time expressing his ideas in a trio without a drummer, because ". . . Without this interplay [between the drummer and other instrumentalists] it is impossible to play most styles of jazz. Moreover, without the drummer I cannot perform Brazilian, Latin and African musical styles as effectively because these musical styles require the propulsion of the drum." Walrath and Cuscuna both argued that the limitation in practice discriminated against forms of American music identified with blacks and latins.

Although that discrimination was undoubtedly behind the restriction, its effects were much broader. Its purpose of discouraging anything but "background music," together with the generality of the legal form in which the regulations were cast, had a tendency, apart from exceptional cases like the piano-bass duets, to inhibit the use of exciting musical forms. Both Jon Pareles and Mike Mikell said that the interest of the music generally rises as the number of instruments increases. Thus the limitation interfered with the natural instrumentation of all sorts of vernacular music, including Bluegrass. Tony Trischka, a famous banjoist, said that he could no longer perform at the Eagle Tavern with his Bluegrass quintet as he had done for years. Bluegrass requires at least four instruments—guitar, mandolin, bass and banjo—to ". . . flesh out the subtle musical nuances of the style. For example, the mandolin functions as a percussion instrument in that it provides the offbeats for the other instruments." In fact, as the Cafe Figaro episode had shown, the regulation was restrictive enough even to interfere with the serious presentation of European classical or modern music, if any establishment chose to try it.

The limitation, Cuscuna and Walrath pointed out, created a continuing *de facto* discrimination against horns, because the most workable form of a trio is piano, bass and drums; thus clubs limited to a trio would tend to work without horns. Mark Morganelli testified that as a trumpeter, he had had the experience of being refused jobs because the club to which he applied was using the basic trio.

We established the lack of adequate channels of communication by starting with David Sheldon's survey of how clubs were using their licenses. He had found only about forty of the ninety-odd cabaret licensees in Manhattan offering live music. Even those places, however, because of the capital they have sunk into their establishments, do not usually hire musicians without a "name," and thus younger, less well-known musicians usually cannot get jobs in them. Jon Pareles pointed out that the situation is actually worse than the figures might indicate:

> There's a larger consideration, too: the effect on American music. New York is the world's center of jazz because of its jazz clubs; jazz has little presence in the record business (less than 6 percent of the market), but survives and evolves as live entertainment. And it is the city's smaller, often unlicensed clubs that keep jazz alive; bigger places tend to book rock bands or groups for dancing.

The younger players, who might have new and unconventional ideas, had to play in the unlicensed places. If they could only play in trios, then, they would not get to express themselves or even learn to play in the larger forms. Cuscuna, Pareles, Glasel, Walrath and Morganelli all noted this pattern. They were in effect saying that the limitation to a trio in small, obscure places was at odds with the entire tradition of learning to play and trading ideas by constantly jamming with others.

Terry Pender, a young mandolin player, described the problems of his group, consisting of guitar, bass, mandolin and violin:

> . . . [The] group is not a loud group. We have a difficult time getting engagements in places that have a cabaret license, because they generally want a band that makes a more aggressive sound than we do. We are paid relatively little in the small clubs where we can get engagements. For [an] engagement . . . at the Eagle Tavern, we were paid 255 dollars for the four of us for the night. We have also played in a club where we were paid 60 dollars and 90 dollars for the band on two separate occasions. In all cases, I believe these payments were percentages of the

house receipts, which indicates, I think, that we do not draw the sort of crowd that a more famous group would draw. We play in small places, not primarily because of the money, but because we cannot generally get hired to play elsewhere, and because we want to play and be heard.

Mikell's was one example of an unlicensed club where little-known performers had an opportunity to try new ideas. Mike Mikell said:

In the past, Mikell's has showcased performers during the week, from Monday to Thursday. These have often been young jazz and rock musicians who have a difficult time getting a hearing if they can't play at Mikell's. Among those who have been showcased are Stuff, a famous rhythm-and-blues quintet, and Whitney Houston, who is now very famous. Most of these performers do not work with a trio and cannot reduce to a trio to play at Mikell's.

The lack of access drove some styles entirely out of town or underground. Relatively unpopular styles, like relatively unknown musicians, cannot get work in licensed clubs. Pareles, Cuscuna and Glasel might well have added small-band swing to Bluegrass and Dixieland in the list of styles that were being shut out. I myself saw this effect on avant-garde jazz as the unlicensed loft jazz spots, often run by musicians, died out. Most club owners, as well as much of the audience, as Michael Cuscuna said, do not understand or like progressive music, and thus avant-garde jazz has had a much more limited hearing in the eighties.

The interest in free expression was thus a relatively easy issue for the plaintiff musicians; more problematic was the issue of the nature of the City's legitimate interest in the regulation. Recent U.S. Supreme Court cases had been concerned frequently with "adult" entertainment, particularly movies. In *City of Renton v. Playtime Theatres*, the Court had held that the problem of discrimination against content could be substantially avoided by the municipality if it could show "undesirable secondary effects" due to the films.[26] Put more simply, if the City of Renton could show that adult movies went along with crime and a decline in retail trade, then it had a sufficient interest to justify zoning even if the secondary effects were connected to the content of the movies as "adult" movies. And so it followed, if New York City could show some important detriment to the "quality of life" from music in restaurants and bars, then it had an argument that might nearly overcome the others; certainly it would tend to make our proof about content-discrimination ineffective.

In *Playtime Theatres* the municipality introduced studies of the economically and socially destructive effects of adult movies on neighborhoods in other cities. Peter LaRoca Sims remarked to me in this connection that he was "offended by having music equated with pornography," but in fact the City was not able to show the equation. We were sure that the City had no studies showing the adverse effects of music on a neighborhood, because if such studies existed we would have heard of them; furthermore, we were virtually certain that there were no such effects. The chief effect of music on urban life, we believed, was to improve it.

All the City had was the Chief Engineer's affidavit about the possibility of "congestion" affecting the "quality of life;" it seemed clear to us that was not enough; as one court had said, ". . . the city must produce more than a few conclusory affidavits of city leaders which primarily contain unsubstantiated opinions and allegations."[27]

Nevertheless, since we were in the treacherous waters of a summary judgment motion, I thought we ought to show that we could prove our side of the case—that music would not cause congestion. I began to interview environmental engineers and consultants; one of the first I encountered was Fred Kent and the Project for Public Spaces. Kent told me, firmly, that he would never undertake to testify along those lines, because the whole basis for the City's zoning policy against "strangers" and "congestion" was wrong-headed. Local neighborhoods deserted and silent at night are not an unqualified good, and busy pedestrian traffic does not lower the "quality of life," he said; thus even if what the City claimed were true, it would not show that music was bad for local neighborhoods. He took the opportunity to say to me pointedly that the legal profession was largely responsible for propagating such ideas and lending them respectability, as I was doing by taking the City's argument seriously.

I was impressed by Kent's position, having encountered similar ideas from William H. Whyte in the past, but I could not make use of it just then. The First Amendment argument at the heart of our case was directed at a discrimination, really an inconsistency, in the City's zoning and licensing; the argument did not give us any good basis to attack zoning policy generally, even if we thought it was rooted in an erroneous theory. The City continued to have a plenary power over its zoning that we could breach only by showing that city regulations violated some strong right in a specific way. Kent's reaction was a sobering comment on how narrow the case really was. We could not, for example, lower commercial rents, nor actually obtain spaces for musicians to play; all we could get a grip on with the means at hand was discrimination against musicians.

A friendly environmental lawyer referred me to Brian Ketcham, a noted engineer who had once been Director of Planning and Implementation for the City's Department of Environmental Protection. His affidavit proved to be the linchpin of our argument against the City's "quality of life" claim. Ketcham said that there were no studies of the relative impact of the presence or absence of entertainment on traffic near restaurants. He went on to say that "there is no relation between the number of musicians who play in a restaurant and the amount of pedestrian and vehicular traffic—that is, the number of people—that will be drawn to the neighborhood." The impact of a restaurant on traffic depends almost entirely on its size—how many people could be accommodated in it. "In my expert opinion, however," he went on, "in a neighborhood which has mixed uses, including restaurants, the presence or absence of entertainment in such establishments does not make a significant difference." Some uses, he said, really do cause a dramatic difference in traffic; among them are fast-food restaurants with rapid turnover, like McDonald's, and dance places, which accommodate most of their patrons standing up.[28]

Ketcham recognized that entertainment in a restaurant might sometimes attract a crowd, but he did not think that it was a generalized problem. As Michael Cuscuna remarked, a club may attract a crowd because of the name recognition of a performer, but small clubs often cannot afford to pay such performers. Ketcham said, ". . . as between two establishments which have the same capacity, one may be more popular, may be filled to capacity more often and thus may generate more traffic; but whether a place is the 'in' place is not generally related to whether it has entertainment nor to the number of musicians who play at the place."

As a matter of fact, the "in" places that caused neighbors to complain usually had no live music at all. During 1988, for example, the Gramercy Park neighborhood complained about a group of watering places that were waking people up at all hours. Chief among them was Cafe Iguana, a Mexican restaurant seating four hundred and located on Park Avenue South, in the same district where twenty years earlier a suit had been threatened against the nightclub at Max's Kansas City. Yet David Sheldon found, after doing another quick survey for the union, that neither Cafe Iguana nor other nearby popular bars had so much as a note of live music. They could cause plenty of ruckus just with canned music and booze. The proprietor of the cafe, who styled herself Mama Iguana, responded to the complaints with words of one who has no zoning worries: "This is the city that never sleeps. Stop trying to put us to bed."[29] Shades of

speakeasy proprietor Texas Guinan! The neighbors would probably have been better off with the nightclub at Max's Kansas
City, long since disappeared.

In our view, then, the City's arguments about traffic congestion were fully as applicable to restaurants and bars generally as
to places that had four-piece bands. They ran afoul of the principle propounded in the *Schad* case, that a municipality cannot
single out live entertainment for restrictive zoning, in the name
of "local" uses and reduced traffic, while ignoring other uses
that have the same effects.

Finally, Ketcham's and other affidavits made it clear that the
ordinance was not narrowly tailored to reach its ends. The City
could more easily control traffic congestion directly by traffic
regulations, or indirectly by limiting the size of restaurants and
bars in local commercial neighborhoods. Thus we pulled the
argument around again to make our point that the best explanation for the restrictions on clubs with music only was that they
discriminated against jazz and other vernacular music because of
ancient and ill-founded prejudices.

Law students in Claudia Angelos' clinic spent the spring term
of 1987 interviewing most of the witnesses, collecting affidavits,
studying regulations in other cities, and drafting legal arguments. In May, as the law school term came to an end, we filed
all the papers with the court, argued the motion, and began to
wait for the decision. In the meantime, the press continued to
oppose or at least question the City's position. The *Times* ran
another op-ed piece by the New School's David Levy attacking
the law, and later editorialized against it.[30]

Among musicians and club owners, the pressure was mounting; the crackdown on the clubs continued. Since Mikell's was
in my neighborhood, I walked by it often in the evening, either
to discuss the case or listen to a set, or both. Both of the Mikells,
Mike and his partner, Pat, were crying the blues; they had gone
into debt, and could not get out of it as long as they were
booking trios. Arnie Lawrence, a saxophonist and one of the
directors of the New School's jazz college program, was trying

to organize a mass refusal to play in New York establishments, from July 1 "until the cabaret licensing law falls."[31] The union was exasperated; their experience with such tactics under Petrillo had not been encouraging. Arnie Lawrence's friend Peter LaRoca Sims set out to convince him that it would never work.

The rest of us were in reality nearly as anxious as Arnie Lawrence. Every few weeks, a group of us, including politicians, musicians and club owners, met in John Glasel's office to talk about what we could do to change the City's mind. As interested in lobbying as ever, the union helped City Councilmember Stanley Michels draft a bill to eliminate the three-musician rule both in the ordinances and the Zoning Resolution.

We were interested in persuading the City if we could, because even if the City's motion was denied, we would still be very far from success; at best we expected to have to go through a trial and win it. In the fall of 1987, Claudia Angelos and I began, with the help of a new group of law students, to think about how we would prepare our case if we won the motion. We started talking again to environmental engineers, to plan in detail how we would prove that small music clubs do not cause an increase in traffic on the streets, or—even more difficult—how it might be a good thing even if they did. We tinkered with a list of city officials who would have to be called as witnesses. As the motion papers waited on Justice Saxe's desk for a decision, the possible aftermath was a depressing prospect.

DECISION

The final action by the court astounded everyone. On January 28, 1988, Justice Saxe declared the entire "incidental musical entertainment" exception unconstitutional. He took the City's motion for summary judgment, turned it on its head, and granted judgment for the plaintiffs, bypassing the need for a trial. He began by accepting our arguments about musical "content" for constitutional purposes:

[The musicians] observe that the content of music cannot be separated from the number of musicians and instruments needed to create a work of art and submit an impressive array of affidavits from various experts to support this argument. It is contended that the three-musician limitation imposed by the City of New York has nearly eliminated certain types of music, such as Dixieland or Bluegrass music. Moreover, it also appears that the three musician restriction has also had a negative impact on jazz music (sic). Thus it is plaintiffs' main contention that the numerical limitation imposed by the ordinance restricts the cultural expression of musical composers and is therefore "content" based. In this regard, they argue that most music cannot be rearranged to be played by only three musicians without losing the essence of the composer's idea. I find that such a three-musician limitation restricts plaintiffs' freedom of expression. . . .[32]

In opposition to this, the City had relied most heavily on the threat of traffic congestion to justify its zoning and licensing restrictions. It was here that they fell through a booby trap in the procedure for summary judgments. The Chief Engineer's affidavit was not enough to prove their case, especially when it was compared with the opinion of Brian Ketcham, a person whose name and reputation most city officials would recognize. The court's opinion said:

The City provides no studies or other evidence to demonstrate that the number of musicians bears any relationship to automotive or pedestrian traffic. In fact, it is the City's position that it need not come forward with a substantial factual basis to support a justification for the three-musician rule. I find that the City has failed to meet its burden in demonstrating any legal basis to justify a three-musician limitation. In searching the record pursuant to CPLR 3212(b) [the summary judgment provisions—ed.] I find that the defendant City of New York has failed as a matter of law to demonstrate a basis for the numerical limitation contained in the incidental music exception to the Cabaret Law.

Although perfectly proper legally, it is rare for a court to grant summary judgment against the party making the motion. We had been quite prepared to see the court do no more than deny the City's motion and let the case go to trial. The law students were overjoyed; they had just helped to win a constitutional case simply by opposing a motion. The court had shaped what might otherwise have been a protracted and messy litigation into one of the shortest I had ever encountered: a year and a half from start to finish. What the judge had done, in effect, was reach out to sweep away in a single act both the zoning and licensing of music in restaurants and bars; he had decided that the system ought to go and got rid of it.

Why was he willing to use a procedural opportunity to abolish the City's licensing scheme? He himself commented two years later:

> I really like to reach the ultimate issues in cases. Another judge might say that I should be more cautious or deferential. But viscerally I feel more comfortable taking a global approach to the whole problem even if I sometimes risk the wrath of the Appellate Division.[33]

There was a rumor abroad that Justice Saxe was systematically "anti-City." Apart from the cabaret case, he had decided a case holding that the City could not force licensed clubs to close at 4 A.M. when state law permitted them to be open until 4:30.[34] And his most celebrated decision undoubtedly was the *Seawall* case, ultimately upheld by the state's highest court, in which he struck down the City's legislation concerning single-room occupancy units (SRO's)—which were often housing for the very poor, for whom the next step was to be altogether homeless. Justice Saxe held that the city law, which required the owners of SRO's, at their own expense, to maintain the units, rent them and not convert them to some other use, was an unconstitutional taking of property without just compensation.[35] Nevertheless, these are only three opinions out of dozens that Saxe has written during his judicial career, among hundreds more cases for which no opinion has been written.

Saxe commented, wryly, that he was surprised to hear that some people might think he was prejudiced against the City:

> Those three are just the "publicity cases." I sat for three years [1986 to 1988—ed.] in a City Part, where cases against the City—mostly tort-damage cases, are presented. I heard that I actually developed a reputation in the plaintiffs' bar for being too pro-City.

And in fact, my research reveals no such anti-City slant in Saxe's opinions generally. In one hundred and ten opinions written in the years 1985 to 1990, we found twenty-eight that concerned the City; seventeen of them were decided in the City's favor.

I asked Justice Saxe if his years at the Department of Consumer Affairs had given him some insight into the regulatory process, enabling him, perhaps, to get beneath merely rhetorical justification for rules. His comment in 1990 was:

> Overall, my view of consumer protection by the City is not favorable. They don't protect much and they ought to stick to weights and measures and the like. They do not prevent fraud or get restitution in most cases.
>
> I do have a jaundiced view of the way the City regulates business. They go much too far in the regulation . . . and I don't think it does much good. I think it just employs people—provides comfortable jobs for lower and middle-level people.
>
> And I object to the way the City bifurcates the regulation—forcing a businessman to go to several places for approval. The licensing and approvals should be joined under one authority.

It is clear that the state of the law before the suit was brought created an opening to assert the rights of musicians, offering only the possibility of a favorable outcome; of course it did not bring it about. The court might still have held that the likelihood of traffic congestion was enough to justify the restrictions in the ordinance. More plausibly, the court could have said that the effect of traffic congestion was a triable issue, and let the case go on through more years of discovery and trial, leaving the parties exhausted, and possibly leading to a compromise. Instead the court shaped those possibilities, both procedural and substantive, to declare the City's justification flimsy and sweep the regulation away. But that victory, in turn, only opened up the social situation to change; it did not actually bring the change about.

CHAPTER 7

THE PROCESS OF CHANGE

THE COURT DECISION

An opinion, even an order, from a court is only a sheaf of papers; it does not affect anything except as people react to it. The attitudes and expectations of people outside the case may be changed by what the court has to say, to be sure. That is especially true of a case like the cabaret case, that received a lot of publicity and involved a public issue about which many people had intense interest and detailed knowledge. The expectations of club owners and musicians had been changed by the mere fact that the case was widely discussed, framed and filed. These interested parties wanted the three-musician rule to be abolished, and the preliminary relief eliminating the discrimination against horns and percussion only whetted their appetite for more. They had finally conceived their problem in terms of right, and promptly began to turn that into an entitlement. When the court reached its final decision, they thought, naturally enough, that the entitlement had been recognized; the reaction was heightened by the speed with which the court had acted. That sort of change, the change in expectation, in the sense of what is due, is real enough; it certainly would have been channeled and deflected in a different direction if the case had been decided the other way.

In another sense, though, an action by a court is effective only when the parties accept the action and change their behavior in response to it. New York procedural law crystallizes part of this process of change by separating the "order" in a case from the court's opinion. Only when the judge signs a proposed order submitted by one or more of the parties does the opinion become effective to force the parties to comply. And, of course, they may not comply. In public-law cases, New York procedure emphasizes the "mere paper" aspect of judicial decisions and orders by providing that the municipality has an automatic stay pending appeal.[1] Thus in our case, the City could have staved off the court's decision, and have gone on enforcing its regulations for the many months until the appeal should be decided, just by filing a notice of appeal—a single sheet of paper with a case-caption, a few dozen words and a lawyer's signature on it.

I was braced for delay. In my experience, the City always appealed; it was so easy. After the City had lost the case brought against the Board of Estimate for violating equal voting rights, for example, the City appealed, even though the borough members of the Board continued to be chosen in a grotesquely unequal manner; the City lost the case in the U.S. Supreme Court without a dissent.[2] Fortunately, the constituency for our decision—the musicians, the club owners, and the press—was not braced for delay. The took the power of the judge more literally; for them, the decision was effective when it was made. Freedom had broken out.

The newspaper critics were delighted; for them the regulations were repressive, and Justice Saxe's decision was the only way to go. Besides, this was a natural story, easy to tell.

They helped to make this a very popular decision. The day after the opinion came down, the *New York Post* ran three stories, one headlined "Strike Up the Band!" another titled "Play All That Jazz," and the third "Cabaret, Comedy Clubs Popping Corks," adding a montage of old headline stories with the caption, "*Post* headlines tell the story of an unpopular law that has been declared unconstitutional." The owner of the Angry Squire was quoted saying "the quality of music is going to be up 100 percent in New York" while Pat Mikell expressed the hope that Mikell's would be able to get out of debt. Vince Giordano, who runs a traditional big band, exclaimed, "I feel like we've landed on the moon! I can't believe we beat the system. This has been like Prohibition." The *Daily News* headline was, "New Cabaret, Old Chum," with a sidebar "Way to go, Judge." The *New York Times* story was cooler, but over the weekend, after running into me and Claudia Angelos, along with a lot of others, celebrating at Mikell's, Jon Pareles wrote a story that sounded the "end of Prohibition" theme again. It quoted me worrying about a possible appeal, but saying, "Eat, drink and be merry." I left out the rest of the adage.[3]

From my point of view, the most important newspaper piece was the *Daily News* editorial "Jammin' with Justice Saxe," with these closing words:

> . . . In other words, it's now constitutional to blow your own horn in New York City. About time, too. Catch you at the next jam session, Justice Saxe. Don't forget to bring that crazy robe.
>
> Meanwhile, anybody in city government who *thinks* about appealing Saxe's ruling should be hooted out of town.[4]

Anybody who had been thinking about it apparently stopped. The City's lawyer called to ask whether we could put off having the actual order submitted and signed; that way he could put off having to appeal. City agencies, recognizing the need for change, he said, had been trying to draft new regulations, including zoning provisions, and he wanted to give them a chance to complete the process. The City would agree not to enforce the old cabaret laws against music as long as the order was suspended and the drafting process went on. This was a very odd arrangement—making the decision effective by making it ineffective on paper—but having the cabaret laws not enforced was superior to having an order, an appeal, and an automatic stay for the City, followed by more enforcement of the old laws. And I couldn't stop city agencies from drafting regulations anyhow.

The compromise was a perfect demonstration that a court decision usually works when the parties decide that it will work.

Despite the City's dreary promise to re-zone, the decision was effective in the clubs. It worked automatically because, as a deregulation no governmental response was needed. Unlike a civil rights decision that restructures an institution such as a prison, a school system or voting districts, the cabaret decision did not require any further input of governmental expertise or money; neither the judge nor anyone in the City needed to exert the slightest effort. To become effective, the decision depended, in philosophical terms, on negative or self-executing rights rather than positive rights. The clubs and the musicians could restructure the club business themselves; all the government had to do was get out of the way.

The step taken by Justice Saxe was not only a decision popular with the press and public, but one that dovetailed with some elite views about the place of law that were fashionable in the eighties. For those who were critical of judicial "activism," arguing that judges who restructure institutions are acting beyond the scope of their skills, and usurping political functions, this should have been a appropriately modest decision, doing no more than establishing rights as against a system of regulation.[5] The judicial move was also consonant with social science opinion favoring deregulation, especially in New York, which was considered by many to be extravagantly over-regulated.[6] Both sets of views have similar roots, favoring *laissez-faire* in civil society, modest government intervention and a conception of rights primarily negative in nature.

The effect on the clubs was varied. Some that had been skirting the law all along found that they could operate more easily. Judy Barnett of J's, at 97th and Broadway, was quoted as saying, "Hallelujah. Thank goodness the law will no longer be making artistic decisions for the people who perform at J's." When I talked to her in 1990, however, she said that J's had never systematically complied with the three-musician rule, although she had received at least one summons for a violation. The difference was that the club could now advertise and get reviews frankly setting forth the size of the groups. The Knitting Factory, in an isolated industrial space on Houston Street east of Broadway, happened to have Sun Ra's seventeen-piece band booked to play the night the owners heard that the law was changed. The booking was ironical, but not deliberate; they had scheduled Sun Ra long before and the ruling made no difference to their policies. Andy Lugris at Visiones on MacDougal Street said that the only difference was that there seemed to be more clubs opening.[7] And I had myself watched Augie's, the tiny place on Broadway near 106th Street where the youngest, least-known musicians came to play, throughout the entire period when the case was pending and after. No change there—still booking quartets, with lots of people sitting in as the night wore on.

To many club owners, though, it made more difference. The Red Blazer Too, one of the very few places in New York that features traditional jazz, had been recently opened on West 46th Street. Vince Giordano, together with others who played the older music, would be there with viable groups. Larry Heller of the West End Bar said that he was about to hire more musicians, as did the Mikells and the owners of the Angry Squire. Garvin's, a restaurant on Waverly Place, said that it would be augmenting its bands.[8]

This was brave talk, which the money pressures of high rents and debts as well as bigger bands would make it difficult to live up to. But there was some solid sign of change as time went on. The Red Blazer Too, the Angry Squire and Garvin's did book more interesting bands. Bradley's often hired more than its traditional piano-bass duets. Supper clubs, like the Fortune Garden Pavilion in Midtown, began to offer jazz. A club at the corner of 105th Street and Broadway adopted the famous old name of Birdland, and Mark Morganelli, one of the plaintiffs in the cabaret case, was managing the music. The Zanzibar and Grill, on Third Avenue at 36th Street, adopted a jungle motif together with jazz and latin music. Rock clubs were opening in the East Village.[9]

In Brooklyn, Teddy's was offering the same solid quintets on weekends that it had had while the case was pending. But there was a lot more music in the borough. Restaurants began to find that small bands increased their clientele, and musicians went to work. One said, "Manhattan club owners want big names to play, but in Brooklyn the younger musicians get a chance to work," and another added, "I find that people in Brooklyn are starved for live entertainment and music in general." Jazz was becoming an accepted art; one of the patrons said, "I find the music very soothing . . . as long as it's jazz or blues, something with a mood to it."[10]

A spirit of mild experimentation prevailed. A restaurant could try out a music policy and see if it worked. The Manhattan Chili Company, on Bleecker Street, began to offer various sorts of "festivals," each organized by a musician. Pianist Joel Forrester, of whom more later, put together a festival of "two-fisted piano" and avant-garde clarinetist Perry Robinson organized a jazz clarinet festival, a real rarity in this age dominated by the saxophone. As part of perestroika and glasnost, a Soviet impresario opened a showcase, one night a week, called Vartan's Bluebird, for Russian jazz musicians. *New York Times* reviewer Peter Watrous wrote, "[t]o become a jazz musician often involves brutal, humiliating encounters with better versed, more experienced improvisers. The Soviet musicians sounded as if they had never run into that sort of heart-stopping challenge."[11] They were going to run into that challenge if they kept their place open long enough in New York.

But the City had still not really accepted the change. While clubs were starting, or expanding, or emerging from the shadows, the City's process of re-drafting the regulations went into gear. The City Planning Department was responding not only to the decision in our case but to the bill that Stanley Michels was pushing for the musicians in the City Council.

THE POLITICS OF ZONING

The Michels bill was originally conceived during meetings in John Glasel's office as an alternate channel to try to change the cabaret laws, before we knew that Justice Saxe was going to hold them unconstitutional as applied to music. The bill proposed to require a license only for clubs that allowed dancing by the patrons, or accommodated over two hundred people; smaller bars and restaurants with music were to be exempt. We argued about whether we ought to try to draft something to cover the licensing and zoning of other forms of entertainment, such as comedy and dance, only to give the project up repeatedly because we knew so little about the social effects of the other forms. If we had not been such a jerry-built group, meeting from time to time and on the fly, we might have contrived to study the problems of other arts and to form a broader coalition with them. But since none of us knew how to go about doing that, we would up writing our exemption just for small places with music.

We had thought this change would at least eliminate the three-musician rule, and at the same time come to grips with the City's claim about traffic congestion. Since we had learned from Brian Ketcham during our case that congestion was caused more by the number of people who could fit in a place than by the presence of entertainment, we thought we could obviate every legitimate objection if we left a licensing system in place for larger establishments. Planners later told me that the figure of two hundred seemed to them low. That only reflected how small the clubs usually are; a capacity of two hundred was larger than any unlicensed club we could think of. The bill also proposed finally to coordinate the licensing with the zoning process by providing that the City Planning Commission could not regulate the zoning of bars and restaurants by forbidding or limiting live music.

After Justice Saxe's decision, Stanley Michels kept pressing his bill as a way of legislating the result of the case and heading off the City's plans to re-zone. The inclusion of the zoning limitations in the bill did have some effect; the bill's occasional appearance on the Council's calendar for a hearing obliged the City Planning Department to finish its drafting and make a proposal for zoning changes. Because planning for land use was the customary preserve of City Planning, the city administration wanted to forestall the Council from any action on zoning.[12]

City Planning officials began to meet with us in 1988 to float trial balloons. To hear them tell it, they had realized for a long time that the provisions about night clubs in the Zoning Resolution were antiquated, and the court decision had finally pushed them to act. In the spring of 1989, City Planning finally unveiled its proposal. It would have created a new category, of music-only clubs accommodating less than 175 people. These establishments were to be allowed only by "special permit" in zones like local (C1) and gilt-edged (C5) commercial districts where clubs had formerly been forbidden. Any restaurant was to be allowed freely to have "accessory music" in the form of background music without a cover charge or show time. Any clubs that accommodated more than 175 or that had dancing was still to be excluded from the forbidden zones. And all this new zoning machinery, of course, was to be piled on top of the cabaret license from the Department of Consumer Affairs, which was still to be required for the discos and the larger music clubs.

This proposal would have been laughable, were it not for the fact that, because the City's money and talent had been spent on it, it was serious. It almost brought us back to 1986—no, even back to 1955, when the "incidental music" exception had crept into the Zoning Resolution. The principal change in this proposal was a provision for a special permit in zones that had been off limits to entertainment under the old law; from the musicians' point of view, that seemed to be no change at all.

In discussions at City Planning, I began by asking wearily why they were perpetuating background music as an exception; that, after all, was what had led to all the constitutional trouble. The Chairperson favored me with a little story. There was a pianist who played in the local restaurant in the neighborhood where she lived on the East Side—had been working there for years. His music was just background, pleasant but not important to the patrons. I had to understand that the Commission did not, of course, want to interfere with that sort of thing.

I asked her what she would make of the situation if the pianist were a genius and attracted people from all over the world to listen to him. She reacted, of course, as though that were an absurd scenario, and I realized we were wasting our time. The Department's people had apparently not even read the decision in the case, or if they had, what the judge said meant nothing to them; they did not see that regulation of the content of music was the bedrock issue on which the whole controversy turned. Artistic and legal issues mattered a lot less now; this was a political fight.

This kind of fight was just the sort of thing the musicians union was good at. As City Planning began to present its proposal to the fifty-nine Community Boards, preparatory to holding a public hearing and then presenting the proposal to the Board of Estimate for approval,[13] John Glasel, Judy West and other union representatives went to community and borough-wide board hearings as often they could manage, constantly explaining the union's opposition. I am not sure how much they persuaded people, but they often enough raised questions in the minds of board members, who are usually suspicious of centralized authority. On some boards, especially in Manhattan, the union had allies to agitate against the proposal.

From time to time, in the effort to get us to cooperate, we were invited to more meetings at City Planning. When I asked the Chairperson why they wanted to require special permits, to be obtained from the Board of Standards and Appeals, for small music clubs in the local and gilt-edged commercial districts, she pointed out that the special permit system was only an extension of one that already existed for "regional" commercial (C2) districts. In those cases, she said, the permits were given out with great ease. The Board acted like greased lightning, she said; it leaned over backwards; and more of the same.

I was surprised that they expected us to be persuaded by this. Before granting a permit, the Board required consultation with the local Community Board, as well as a statement concerning the effect on environmental quality. The permit was for a limited time, and the Board often demanded and received concessions, as for example, on the hours of operation and the number of instruments that could be played. Although this was not technically a Uniform Land Use Review (ULURP) procedure, it was almost indistinguishable in practice and nearly as cumbersome. It was, in fact, quite similar to the procedure through which City Planning was now slogging, going to the Community Boards for approval of its zoning text amendments.[14]

According to City Planning, the Board has received only five requests for such club permits, granting four, in the two and a half years before June, 1987; none in Manhattan, and none for music-only clubs. I thought I could see why; the process was arcane, expensive and unlikely to be successful in a great many cases. For clubs that seated more than 175 persons, moreover, the City proposed in addition to require a cabaret license from the Department of Consumer Affairs.

I did not have to imagine how convoluted this double-licensing process could be; there was a case unfolding on the West Side at the very time that City Planning was proposing its zoning changes. In the basement of a twelve-story building on the corner of 79th Street and Amsterdam Avenue, formerly the Hotel Lucerne and now turned into private apartments, a group of partners was trying to open a supper club with dancing. There was already a restaurant at the ground-floor level; this group wanted to soundproof and use the basement. A special permit was required because the corner was in a regional (C2) commercial district; it is in fact a busy corner, with two-way traffic on 79th Street.

In the summer of 1988, the partners, who wanted to call their place the Crane Club—apparently a nostalgic joke on the name of the now-defunct Stork Club—applied for approval to the Community Board. They had to appear before the Board on no fewer than four occasions, and as time wore on, people in the neighborhood, but not actually living in the building, grew more agitated at the prospect of a "disco." The Board finally approved the proposal with stringent conditions, including a limitation to a very small dance floor, doormen and valet parking for the patrons, a "reservations only" policy, limits on hours, and finally, the "club to be operated as a supper club and not as a discotheque as those terms are commonly used."

The Crane Club then sought and received a statement from the Department of Environmental Protection that the club would have "no significant effect" on the environment, provided it was soundproofed. Subsequent tests showed that the soundproofing had eliminated the noise above the basement level.

In February, 1989, represented by Norman Marcus, former counsel to the City Planning Commission, the club began its application to the Board of Standards and Appeals (BSA) for a special permit. Organized chiefly by the landowner across Seventy-ninth Street, the "neighbors" came to protest the permit; the case-record contains no evidence that anyone living in the building where the club was actually to be located ever objected. One of the objectors said, "We are not opposed to music. We are not opposed to clubs." What they were opposed to was discotheques, no doubt envisioning ugly crowds of stoned young people. The partners and their lawyers kept saying that the place was to be a quiet supper club, quite "up-scale," as Norman Marcus put it; the objectors flatly refused to believe it. After hearing the case on five occasions, the BSA finally approved the permit, finding that Amsterdam Avenue and 79th Street could accommodate the increase in traffic, and setting restrictions which, although less detailed than those of the community board, still included valet parking, doormen, and a limitation on hours. The approval was limited to one year. The neighboring landowner and others tried and failed to get the Board of Estimate to reverse the BSA.

Armed with the precious permit, the club began the process of getting a cabaret license from the Department of Consumer Affairs, this time represented by a different lawyer, Robert Bookman, formerly a lawyer for the Department. The neighbors, including the landowner across the street, started a suit to reverse the decision of the BSA, in the process obtaining a stay of administrative proceedings. Bob Bookman had to get the stay lifted in order to start his application for the license. And for that, of course, he needed current fire and electrical inspections, leading to further delay.

In February of 1990, the court sent the matter back to the BSA to ensure that the dance floor was limited in size and that the owners were trustworthy. Bookman was predicting that it would be nearly two years before the Crane Club got its license.[15]

I was impressed by the resiliency of the Crane Club partners. It was difficult for me to picture anyone having the patience, much less the resources, to withstand the process; certainly I could not imagine most jazz clubs being able to do it. It is true that an application for a pure music club might not provoke so much opposition as a dance club. Jazz clubs are not the *bêtes noires* they once were, as the decision in our case and the process of zoning change was showing us; discos seem to have taken their place as the nightmare of a peaceful neighborhood. But even at best, this was a complex process, requiring expert assistance. And it is likely that some self-appointed keeper of property values, especially a nearby landowner, would decide in any case that it would be better if the club did not exist.

The only jazz club I knew of for which a special permit had been sought and obtained was Sweet Basil, on Seventh Avenue South in Greenwich Village. One of the partners, Mel Litoff, carried through the applications in the early eighties. But Sweet Basil was a club that had already existed for years without having got its papers in order, it was a C2 (regional commercial) district that had had many clubs over the years, and it was surrounded by commercial uses that were also related to entertainment. Substantial local opposition did not develop. And Litoff says that the Consumer Affairs people were more obliging and helpful with the licensing process at that time than they were later; they let the club continue operating while the applications were pending. When he and his partners took over Lush Life, a couple of blocks down Bleecker Street, its papers were in even more of a mess, and they were not able to make a successful application.[16]

Special permits were intended, as Norman Marcus put it, "to deal with the externalities of the use—such as crowds, noise and traffic—in a sensitive way."[17] But the process, as he pointed out, was just as difficult for a club as it was for a forty-story building; in fact, it was worse if a cabaret license was required. For music-clubs, the expansion of the special-permit procedure to local (C1) and gilt edged (C5) commercial districts would have amounted virtually to a law without users, a paper procedure with which hardly anyone would comply.

As I heard about the musicians union resisting the City Planning Department at the Community Board meetings, I wondered why City Planning was putting itself through this. They were faced with a court decision, widely accepted as a wise one, declaring their old system dead. They even claimed that they agreed with it, to the extent they thought the old system was outdated. The state of music in the clubs during the period of more than a year since the decision had been in effect was the best possible argument we could have had; it was a laboratory of what would happen in case of deregulation. Clubs were open in formerly forbidden zones. There were some noise complaints that were being dealt with by summonses from the Department of Environmental Protection. There were no resulting crowds or traffic—hardly a trace of the zoning problems the City had offered as justification for its old rules, and was offering for its new proposals. These months in fact afforded the only empirical experience that anyone had ever had about what the effect would be of the abolition of the old system of licensing and zoning. Why not just let the situation alone?

I made these arguments and asked this question at the City Planning Department many times. The only answer I ever heard was that failing to regulate "would not be land-use planning." I knew that opaque phrase was a code for something else, but for months I could not quite see what it was.

The City has for years used its zoning provisions as tools for bargaining with developers. As Paul Goldberger has remarked, the regulatory impulse, to impose some planned control over development in the city, has been in tension with the economic impulse, to permit as much freewheeling growth as possible.[18] So the City has used its zoning powers to obtain concessions— often called "give-backs"—from developers. Some of them were automatic—"as-of-right" as they are called—built into the Zoning Resolution; for example, until recently a developer had a right to increase the size of his building if he provided an amenity such as a plaza—one of those plazas so often bleak and shunned by passers-by. But those automatic bargains, now much more limited, only express bluntly a characteristic that runs through the process of zoning approvals, appearing even more strongly in the discretionary decisions. The ULURP procedure, for example, affords a number of opportunities for bargaining. The Community Board may ask for concessions from the developer which may be thought to "benefit" the local community, at least in the short run. For example, some years ago, a health facility received approval from a Community Board in Brooklyn for a nursing home only in return for a commitment not to allow mental patients. City Planning may ask for other concessions in connection with the Environmental Impact Statement.

Special permits, which could be given by the Board of Standards and Appeals for uses such as clubs in some commercial zones, have been a chief means of retaining some control, of getting something back for the city from hungry developers.

The Crane Club case offered a number of minor examples of the opportunities in the BSA procedure for bargaining.

While the districts and uses defined in the Zoning Resolution and set out on the City zoning map were intended to create a loose plan, or anyway a set of channels, for development, the bargaining process really determined what the City would receive from developers in individual cases. Each project, as it passed through ULURP or some similar process of approval, was worked out separately between City Planning and the developer. Thus City Planning officials much preferred special permit procedures, usable for bargaining, to as-of-right procedures; they probably even preferred them to absolute interdictions, such as those that had existed against clubs before the court decisions. In those cases, there was no room to extract something from the proponents of a project in return for permission.

What City Planning had seen in the cabaret decision, then, was an opportunity for increased governmental control, to get more of a grip on what happens in the neighborhoods, and shape it by means of give-backs. The last thing they wanted was to let an important city resource, such as music was said to be, to pass to an as-of-right status.

This was understandable, from the City's point of view. Developers were taking advantage of the City through the as-of-right procedures; studies showed that builders had gained much more than they had given away in plazas through the as-of-right system. The city had not done much better through special permits, at least for amenities such as public areas at the street level in new buildings, but control over such decisions at least offered some hope of obtaining more benefits and better planning.[19] No doubt it seemed perfectly appropriate to get something back from entrepreneurs who were able to take advantage of the enormous value of New York City land.

The problem is that most of the owners of clubs with music are not entrepreneurs in the sense that City Planning had in mind. Even the very best find that it is a marginal business. Max Gordon found that he had always to be at his club, pay attention to the artists, the food and the customers. Mel Litoff of Sweet Basil, who told Stuart Troup of *Newsday* how running the club required knowledge of the music and the business, still said, "there is no big money in it." The late Bradley Cunningham, proprietor of Bradley's, who said that running his place was "a never-ending thrill," also wearily remarked, looking back to the beginnings of his club, "It would be more of a venture now than I would be ready for." Those who have a flair can find ways to stretch the potential of a club. Michael Dorf and Robert Appel, the young men who run the Knitting Factory on Houston Street, have had Knitting Factory music festivals in other cities in this country and Europe, they have sponsored some "Live at the Knitting Factory" records, and there is a radio program broadcasting their music. Although all this makes the Knitting Factory better known, and attracts more people, it does not make them rich; these ventures net them nothing or next to nothing.

Gordon, Litoff, Cunningham and the Knitting Factory partners have been among the most dedicated and well-organized of club owners. For many proprietors, even if they love the music, hiring a band is something that is added on to the booze business, or less frequently the restaurant business. As Felice Kirby of Teddy's in Brooklyn says, "We were looking to appeal to somebody besides the drunks." Gus Cualtas, the proprietor of Augie's, on Broadway near 106th Street, ran it as a neighborhood bar for years, and gradually let young musicians play. Now they play there all the time. Similarly, the Penn Place Pub, on Eighth Avenue near 28th Street, as we shall see in the next chapter, renewed its music policy because musicians who lived nearby started to use it as a place to play. For a generation at least, this has been the way such places get started; the Five Spot and the Half Note were originally not very different.

In the eighties, some of the clubs have added music because, squeezed by the real estate market, they are hoping to make that extra bit of money that will enable them to stay in business. Often they do not succeed. Clubs went out of business all the time in the eighties, unable to meet the rent and then unable to find newer, more reasonable locations. Sutton's supper club in Harlem closed when the rent was raised; even Eddie Condon's, an old, established club, could find no other location after it was pushed out by a new hotel because, as one of the proprietors said, "the economics weren't right."[20]

The proprietors are typically small saloon keepers who might like to have music—if it does not cost them too much; who would venture even to have something that might be called a "club"—if it does not cost them too much. They are just hoping to make a few extra dollars, please their patrons and themselves. In some cases, they are only experimenting with the music, ready to drop it if it is too expensive; they may pay little or nothing to the musicians. They are unable to withstand a complex system of permits and licenses, with its attendant mysteries and legal fees.

Needless to say, they are unorganized and unable to press their interests as a group, insofar as they have any. Although there is a New York Cabaret Association, recently organized by some owners of large nightclubs and discotheques, the clubs continue to be saddled with an array of zoning and licensing problems partly because they have never formed common cause to resist them. The re-zoning of music had been precipitated by the musicians, who were relatively well-organized, rather than by the clubs themselves; thus the clubs hardly got a chance, before the formal hearings on the proposals, to explain how much beyond their capacities the special permit and licensing systems were.

THE CHANGE IN ADMINISTRATION

At one of our City Planning meetings to discuss the zoning proposals, the Chairperson announced that she had to leave no later than six o'clock; she had tickets to hear the Guarneri Quartet at Alice Tully Hall. A music lover! Although I am an admirer of Steinhardt, Tree and Company, I couldn't help thinking that if she had had tickets to hear the David Murray Quartet, or if the Guarneri Quartet had been booked at Sweet Basil, we would quickly be able to find our way out of this zoning mess.

Something like that finally happened. In June, 1989, the Manhattan Borough Board, headed by David Dinkins (at that time the borough president) rejected City Planning's zoning proposal.[21] Dinkins liked jazz, and anyhow the board did not think the proposal was in Manhattan's interest. City Planning was not of course bound by the decisions of any of the boards; but there was some danger that the proposal might fail at the Board of Estimate, on which the borough presidents also sat.

City Planning began to trim its sails to the wind. The proposal was re-drafted in the summer of 1989 to permit music as of right in clubs seating up to two hundred people, in all commercial districts. Wonderful! Exactly what we wanted.

Except—it was limited to Manhattan. In all the other four boroughs, special permits were to be required. Like a country boy under the spell of big-city flimflam artists, I was impressed that City Planning would attempt to put across such a bald political compromise and call it "land-use planning." I wouldn't have had the nerve, myself. But they talked of viewing Manhattan as an "entertainment center," and the other boroughs as—well—different. I thought about how difficult it is to change the zoning text, and how this particular ill-considered compromise was about to create for the foreseeable future a legally enforceable difference between music in Manhattan and everywhere else.

Club owners from the outer boroughs were incensed. Felice Kirby from Teddy's came to a hearing at the Board of Estimate to make an eloquent plea against it. Local 802's David Sheldon also testified:

> It is not only musical entertainment that the CPC proposes to quarantine, it is culture. Each of the many communities within the City nurtures within it music, and musicians. Here as everywhere else, music is not a postcard attraction, but a part of people's lives. It is

music that people enjoy here as they do everywhere else, not only as a night on the town, or as an occasion to mark a marriage and a celebration, but more often just for a few hours out of the house. There's no law against it. Yet.[22]

Sheldon's words made me think about how most of the music of ethnic communities in New York, drawn from Russia and elsewhere in Eastern Europe, from the Mediterranean and the Caribbean, is played outside Manhattan. Although I know relatively little about it, I was fairly sure that the City knew little more and cared even less. Here was true arrogance.

During the fall of 1989, David Dinkins received the Democratic nomination, and was then elected as New York City's first black mayor. The musicians union had campaigned vigorously for him and knew people on his transition team who liked jazz music and understood the issue. As a jazz fan who had already once taken a position against the City's proposal, the mayor-elect, we were sure, would not approve the City Planning's proposal—if we could just get him to pay attention to it. The least we might do is get final consideration put off until the new administration could study it.

But the City Planning people were determined to put the plan across if they could. They had it on the calendar of the Board of Estimate for January 11, 1990, immediately after the new administration came in. The union's people and I were telephoning people in the mayor's office, trying to get them to turn the agency around.

Finally, it happened. The hearing before the Board of Estimate was adjourned. City Planning was going to write a proposal to allow "musical entertainment" as of right in all commercial zones in all the boroughs. There was just one problem: The City had already made the long march through the Community Boards on its previous proposal. No one had the stomach to make the trek again with the new one. Suddenly, the change in political and legal strategy became so rapid that I could barely take it in. Somebody at the City decided that if the order in our case were in effect, the new draft would simply be a change to bring the zoning text into line with the law, and would not require another trip through the Community Boards. Practically overnight, after two years of adjourning the signing of the order in the case, the City presented the final paper to Justice Saxe and got it signed.

City Planning did decide that they needed the votes of three-quarters of the Board of Estimate, the usual way of legitimizing decisions in controversial cases. Elizabeth Holtzman, the new Comptroller, balked at accepting the proposal. One of her aides, who had once been a student in one of my classes, said suspiciously, "I can't believe Chevigny accepted anything so discriminatory."

He meant that the proposal did nothing for anybody but musicians. As City Planning had narrowed it, the proposal no longer aided comedy, or dancing as a performance, not to speak of social dancing. Because the fight was led by musicians, it was distorted from the point of view of the clubs as well as of arts other than music. During our discussions in John Glasel's office, we had given up trying to include comedy and dancing within the purview of our proposal, because we knew so little about the zoning effects of dancing, much less of comedy. The lack of organization among the clubs had had its effect; if I had had any request from a comedy club, indeed from the representatives of any of the arts, for that matter, we could have reworked the proposal. I never had such a request. We just carried out the fight as best we could on behalf of musicians. The result was that in the final proposal, City Planning had to add a footnote that it was working on parallel zoning proposals for other sorts of entertainment.

In February, 1990, the Board of Estimate approved a zoning text change to permit music as of right in bars and restaurants in commercial zones everywhere in the city. The licensing provisions were not rewritten, so that the court's decision against them was in effect. Local 802 threw a big party in the cavernous basement of the Village Gate, where an older man in a three-piece suit played the flugelhorn like an angel. It was John Carisi; I had never heard him play, and up to that point I had no idea what had happened to him.

Later, I looked back over the case to see how the thinking of the new administration differed from that of the Koch administration. The City's about-face concerning the signing of the final order in our case was a rich and ambiguous signal. During the two years after Justice Saxe's decision, the City had put off the order on the excuse that the City did not want to have to appeal and that City Planning was going through the process of getting new zoning regulations approved. Now it had turned out that, of course, the City was not obliged to appeal; but more important, it appeared that once the court order was signed, City Planning did not have to go through the harassing approval process for its regulations. So why had the order been put off in the first place? There seemed to be no viable answer except that the previous administration was trying to neutralize, rather than carry out, the court's decision through the drafting process. The change in "legal strategy" about the final order in fact embodied a change in policy.

Barabara Fife, the deputy mayor who was chiefly responsible for managing the change, explained the underlying change in the City's thinking:

> We considered the problems of disruptive clubs—we thought that problem was largely from discos. We wanted to be responsive to the problem of noise and disruption, but not at the expense of other things in the city.
>
> New York has a special relation to live music. Jazz is a signature of the city. It is something the mayor is proud of and enjoys—but this decision was not oriented that way. We want to encourage live musicians, and we can't predict what styles they will be working in, so we can't

choose which to prefer. For example, in Russian neighborhoods, they play Russian music.

The city needs a reasonable number of jobs for musicians. This is part of our general commitment to a new economic development—not just white-collar and financial and real estate development. Maybe there has been too much emphasis in that direction, so that when the market slipped, it turned out we had too much of our economy invested there. We need new kinds of economic life—more diverse jobs for young people, in more diverse neighborhoods. This decision was part of that.[23]

CHAPTER 8

THE LIVES OF MUSICIANS

Phil Schaap of the West End Bar says:

> The crackdown of the mid-eighties was a graver and more destructive period in the nightclub scene than most people realize. The reason for that was that it was a negative deflection in a diminishing market. . . . It ended the lower-priced nightclub in New York. You still have the freebie—the mere dive. But the sort of club that the West End was an excellent representative of disappeared and hasn't returned. The West End is not doing well now, and its jazz policy may not make it.
>
> There was a transition in jazz nightclub life, parallel to the ups and downs of the fight against the cabaret code. But you change something, and then you turn a lightbulb on in 1988 and say "go back to 1984"—you can't do it. You never can do it. In 1948, they could not go back to '44—they could not bring back big-band dancing after World War II.
>
> The crackdown broke a continuity that might have been able to lift the income of the lower-priced club.

Peter Watrous of the *New York Times* is also gloomy:

> The loosening of the law just coincided with a damping down of the clubs through real estate prices. The prices drove avant-garde clubs out of business. It is *somewhat*

THE LIVES OF MUSICIANS ■

easier for jazz clubs, because it is a little easier for them to raise money. But most of the new ones are barely succeeding. Even the Knitting Factory is on the edge—they charge such a small amount to get in the place.

The situation is certainly touch and go. One evening in May, 1990, Mikell's just does not open. Papers blow past and pile up against the door. I can't get anybody on the telephone, but in June, I run into Pat Mikell on Broadway on her way to look for a job. Their lease ran out, and the landlord wanted to raise the rent from fifteen hundred to forty-eight hundred dollars a month; his real estate taxes went up, he said. Besides, the Mikells never escaped from the debts that were held over from the period of trios. Some of their creditors tried to take over the business—threatened them and insulted Mike Mikell. The Mikells reported them to the district attorney and declared bankruptcy. I mutter that it is terrible, terrible—but in reality I am unable to say how shocked and saddened I am.

I am beginning to wonder whether this is one of those cases that the defendants let you win because there is nothing left to take; they have wrought so much damage that it costs them nothing to give you the satisfaction of winning.

Perhaps not quite. Phil Schaap also says:

> I think the Fortune Garden Pavilion wouldn't have opened if you hadn't won that case. I don't think the West End would have gone back to having a jazz policy . . . Birdland wouldn't have happened; J's wouldn't have happened. The Red Blazer Too would not have reopened. The Cajun never would have happened. It allowed an opportunity to recover the damage. Did we fully recover the scene as of 1984? I don't think so. I think there was damage done; I think of the places that didn't reopen. Like Lush Life—that's the biggest jazz club to completely fail. If the Blue Note had had to continue competing with Lush Life, it might not have

created this "rich people only" atmosphere—where only one club exists that can afford to have certain acts.[3]

Many musicians, especially those who had a routine established long ago, are often not conscious that the change did much of anything. The clubs are and have always been a bewildering world of inadequate pay, sometimes unreasonable bosses, noisy patrons. The legal problems were barely noticeable as something separate; they were just part of the life. When the legal problem changed, the life did not change very much.

Many established musicians would not be likely to play the places that have recently opened or added music. When I spoke to Barry Harris, one of the deans of modern jazz piano, he had just finished playing a weekend with his trio at the Blue Note on West Third Street. He is aware that there is another little club—Visiones—down on the corner of MacDougal, and he thinks it is a good sign. But he does not go to work there.

In some cases, musicians had been playing in places that were illegal, but getting by. There is no particular reason the artists should have known of the status in the first place, or note any change. The avant-garde reed player Henry Threadgill said that he had not played these new places: "I play the same places I always played." One of them is the Knitting Factory, where he was booked to play with Flute Force as part of the 1990 jazz festival; the change in the legal status of the Knitting Factory is invisible because it has not affected the club's policies.[4]

Some established musicians who had spearheaded the move at the union to attack the law are a little disappointed. Sonny Fortune tells me that, although he is now able to play at Birdland and has just finished a gig at Bradley's that was very well-advertised—the New York Times called him a "bruising improviser"—the change has not resulted in the explosion of demand for music that he and others had hoped for. "But it is good for the younger cats. They should set up an organization and try to convince owners that music is the way to go."[5]

Vibraphonist Warren Chiasson, one of the plaintiffs in the case, is less disappointed, perhaps because, under the discrimination against instruments and the three-musician rule, the vibraphone had always been one of the first to go. Since the change, Chiasson has had a lot more gigs, for example at Birdland, the Fortune Garden Pavilion, and Zanzibar and Grill, which is right across Third Avenue from his apartment. Even so, he says, the economic squeeze on the clubs is so great, that a lot of them are still using trios, an arrangement that sometimes leaves him out. There is the now classic trio form of bass, guitar and vibes, however, made famous by Red Norvo, that Chiasson has used at the Fortune Garden.[6]

Some established musicians have long since given up hope of making much of their living from the New York clubs. Peter LaRoca Sims practices law, although on a Sunday afternoon in May, 1990, he used the club Visiones to showcase an excellent band with trumpeter Claudio Roditi and saxophonist Dave Liebman; he was sure the gig was not going to make money, but he felt that it was worth it. Barry Harris, who had experience with the cabaret law at his Jazz Cultural Theater, devotes much of his time to teaching. Many others play a lot of the time elsewhere in the country, particularly at jazz festivals, or abroad. It is, after all, a way of making in a few weeks or even days the kind of money that it would take months to make in the clubs. Henry Threadgill, who devotes part of his time to composition, says that he is in Europe half the time; and at the time I spoke to Junior Mance he had just returned from a tour of Japan with other pianists. Jack Walrath, the trumpeter who gave evidence in our case after his septet was cut to a trio at the Whippoorwill, says that the change has not made much difference in his work; he plays often at festivals or out of the country, as he has for some time.

Among the most popular of younger jazz musicians are the Harper brothers, Winard and Philip, who lead a quintet on drums and trumpet. After playing places like Birdland in 1989, their record album became popular, and they were booked into the Bottom Line, which otherwise rarely offers jazz at all. Philip was quoted in the *New York Times*:

> Though jazz is an American art form created right here in America, most of the money we've made has been in Europe and Japan. . . . I hope the music doesn't slip out of our hands like so many other things. When you think of cars, you don't think American anymore. Now it's Toyota. I hope it doesn't come down to where we have to move over there to make a living.[7]

For some musicians, the sense of liberty is important. Carol Britto, an American pianist who had become something of a celebrity as a jazz musician in Canada, came to New York in 1984 and rebuilt her career. She is now admired as a band pianist as well as a solo or duo pianist. She had experience with the three-musician limitation, both at the Cajun in 1987, when a Dixieland sextet had suddenly to turn itself into a trio, and at the West End Bar. She says it has not really made much difference to her personally, as a pianist, but adds:

> I resented the situation—the law telling the musicians what to play, and telling people what they can hear. I see drums in the Knickerbocker and Bradley's, now. If I work with a bass, I might not want a trio, but I like it that I can suggest to the Knickerbocker that we play as a trio. It is nice to know you have the right to play as you please.

Peter Bernstein, a spirited young guitarist who was worked regularly at Augie's on Broadway near 106th Street, says, "It makes a difference in the respect you get and what you feel. The restrictions were bad, and were not good for the music. It is important to feel you can play as you want."[8]

Indeed, it is to the young and lesser-known musicians that the change makes the most difference. The traditional ways of learning to play, of working with others, of building up a repertoire, and of gradually getting known have changed very little. The obscure clubs—"freebies," as Schaap calls them, usually with no cover or minimum for the music, and with correspondingly little to give the musicians—are important as places to work, to jam and practice constantly, and finally to be heard. The slightly better-known clubs are important as places that may book musicians on their merits, even when they do not have a "name." Peter Watrous recounts the progress of the guitarist Bill Frisell, "who has become an exceptional, distinctive player, mixing rock, country and jazz styles and presenting them all under a great wash of electronic sound." After graduating from the Berklee music school in Boston, he played with other avant-garde musicians in places in Soho in the seventies and eighties, and joined a trio with the jazz drummer Paul Motian. They played at Visiones, and Frisell frequently appeared at the Knitting Factory. In 1990, he was having occasional dates at the Village Vanguard, the oldest of the established clubs. Frisell said:

> I was really nervous the last time I played there. There's such a history to the place. It's a heavy vibe on it. I was worried that we'd alienate people and be too far out. But somehow it really worked out great. The sound in there is perfect. We didn't use much amplification. . . . We played really soft, and when we did play loud, the room handled that, too. With the history, and the sound, and the chance to play six nights in a row, working at the Vanguard is like a dream come true.

Like Frisell, many of the younger musicians now come from the colleges that teach jazz, rock and other styles of contemporary music. Surprisingly, there was no such institution in New York City until 1985 when Arnie Lawrence, a saxophonist, and David Levy established one at the New School for Social Research, in the Parsons School of Design. The school makes its students better-trained musicians than their predecessors, Arnie Lawrence says, but it does not change their need for places to play and get a hearing.

Among them has been Jesse Davis, a husky black alto saxo-phonist with a strong rhythmic attack reminiscent of Charlie Parker. I often heard him leading a quartet on weekends at Augie's in 1989 and 1990. On Broadway near 106th Street, Augie's is basically a hangout for neighborhood regulars and Columbia and Barnard students. With ten tables inside, and a few more outside on hot summer nights, it is so small that there is no sound system at all; the listener is in immediate contact with the music. Although the place has no piano, Davis has excellent keyboard players who bring their own electric instru-ments, most recently a young woman from Japan, Junko Onishi.

The band has been uneven. People come to sit in all the time, and sometimes they are not sure what they are doing, or their style does not fit in with the others. There is some implied "cutting"—musical competition—going on among the saxo-phone players, encouraged by Davis' aggressive style. The group plays Monk's "Rhythm-a-ning" now and then; one night a young tenor saxophonist played a solo closely derived from the one I had heard Johnny Griffin play more than thirty years ago, that had been captured on a live recording.

Although proprietor Gus Cualtas has perennial financial prob-lems, and the musicians get paid by passing the hat, Augie's has become part of a chain of places for musicians to jam. Arnie Lawrence described going to play with and listen to his students and ex-students at the West End, where there was a regular weekly Tuesday jam session, and then passing on to Augie's. He says, "When you walk in there, there's such a good feeling. The musicians are having a good time. They were handing the bass around to different players—and you know how musicians are about their instruments. These kids get better, because there is a scene like when Bird and Monk were playing."

Peter Bernstein, who often led the group on weeknights, said, "There are so few places where conditions are good to play. If you can get the same guys together, you can use Augie's to rehearse and play. I've met most of the musicians I know there.

Many of the people who play other places in New York come there."[10]

In recent months, the musicians who played there were getting better known in New York. Junior Mance, who had taught Jesse Davis in his classes at the New School, hired him for a quartet at the West End. Janet Solesky, a jazz promoter, got Davis's own quintet a showcase, to which the press was invited, on a Saturday night at MK's, an enormous cavern on lower Fifth Avenue housed in a former temple of commerce, perhaps a bank, with marble walls and thirty-foot ceilings, now gilded.

It is a licensed nightclub, isolated in a neighborhood deserted at night like most such places under contemporary conditions, with a disco downstairs, a bar and music space at the ground level, and a restaurant upstairs. The band is essentially the same as at Augie's, with the addition of a tenor sax, except that Junko Onishi is playing a magnificent grand piano instead of her electric keyboard. They play bop standards, and everyone seems to like them. People come up from downstairs to listen, dressed for dancing like peacocks, but it would of course never occur to anyone to dance to this band. Janet Solesky has arranged a similar showcase for Peter Bernstein the next Saturday. Later in the summer, many of these musicians play in bands at the JVC jazz festival as well.

Among those who passed through the New School's jazz program was Virginia Mayhew, an alto saxophonist who came to New York from the West Coast in 1987 to complete her degree at the school. She liked the program so well, and had such hopes of making connections in New York that she persuaded her colleague, trumpeter Rebecca Franks, to join her. Jazz has never been kind to women musicians; while the occasional pianist has been tolerated, it would be rare for two horn players to succeed. The three-musician rule made it even more difficult. Mayhew and Franks did not get any real work until Justice Saxe struck down the law. Immediately after the change, Arnie Lawrence got them a "gig over on West 28th Street, Beaubern

Cafe. . . . This place has been there for years. The guy loves jazz. He gave us a gig there two nights a week for two and a half months, and that was enough for us to get our library together to the point that we could play in some other clubs. Most people don't want to rehearse unless there is a gig."[11]

They have been working every since. Stuart Troup followed their development enthusiastically in his *Newsday* column.[12] By the summer of 1990, they had played one of the experimental Monday nights at the Blue Note and were getting ready for an engagement at J's. Their steady gig, three nights a week, was at the Penn Place Pub, a little bar a few doors up Eighth Avenue from the location of Barry Harris' old Jazz Cultural Theater, still dark and unoccupied—a monument to unreasonable rents— almost three years after it closed. They say they got the job by telling the proprietor that the place ought to have a little music. Apparently it has had music before, because there is a piano in the back behind the banquettes and the formica tables, so out of tune as to be almost unusable.

On a Tuesday night, they play as a quartet, without the piano. They play Miles Davis' "Airegin," a fast bop classic, and "Honeydew," a sinuous Latin blues written by Franks. Then we hear yet another version of Monk's "Rhythm-a-Ning." I listen, as I always do, for the quotations from Johnny Griffin, but I hardly hear them in Virginia Mayhew's solo. She plays a thoughtful alto, making the piece her own. As they play, a group of musician friends come in with Chinese food in containers, sit down and order beer, waiting for a chance to talk and perhaps sit in.

Musicians recognize the value of the more obscure clubs, even as they complain about them. Bobby Sanabria, a drummer well-known in latin bands who leads his own latin-jazz septet, Ascension, says:

> There are more places to play, especially jazz—not so much latin music. Cats from the studio, like on David Letterman, want a chance to play music they have written, to express themselves. Or a cat from a band like

Spyro Gyra will play with his own band in Visiones. These clubs that don't pay that much bread are still places to play. You've got to be able to do things for publicity and build your reputation.

Some of these jazz clubs are getting away with murder, with what they pay the cats. But at least you don't have the government coming down with some bullshit.[13]

Bob Belden is a young reed player, a veteran of Woody Herman and other big bands. He called me in 1986, shortly after the case was filed, when he was being refused jobs at the West End Bar and other unlicensed clubs, to ask if there was anything I could do for him. Because there was nothing I could do except what I was already doing, I did not talk to him again until after the zoning fight was over. When I called to ask whether all of it had made any difference to him, he said:

Make a difference! Let me tell you. I had some charts I had written for a fifteen-piece band. After the decision I dusted them off and got a band together. We played a Monday in Visiones—that's big-band night—February 9, 1989. After one set, we got a record offer. We got a job playing the Paris jazz festival in October, 1990.

There is more happening, now, because more clubs are open. There is a tremendous expansion of the music. A lot of big bands have emerged because of the law.

We are never paid much of anything in these places. My big band works for twenty dollars a person. There are no health benefits—we will never get any benefits in these places. But it is very important that you can use these clubs as a showcase. New York is a symbol—if you want to make it, you have to come here.

As a result, nobody tries to make a living just in Manhattan. Everybody tries to use the clubs as a showcase and then play Europe. You don't hear the well-known musicians very often in New York because they are working in Europe.[14]

Later Belden reflected on the change:

> Once the musicians won, they couldn't believe it—I couldn't believe it. But it also made me angry. I realized how meaningless the law had been. We didn't have to have a cabaret law—it had never made any sense to have it.
>
> I think my problem in 1986 happened because we were at the end of an effort to make Manhattan completely gentrified. It was the hottest time of the highest rents. And they wanted to get rid of these clubs.

The hard question for me, I said, was to understand what had changed the minds of city officials. Belden said:

> I have been reading a lot about censorship. This was a system of censorship, and the musicians were forced to censor themselves. I think it changed because jazz is considered hip and intellectual. It no longer means drug addicts—it's a guy in an Armani suit. He's playing what they teach in the schools. Jazz is a safe commodity. It doesn't have dirty lyrics—it usually doesn't have lyrics at all.

Belden has put his finger on a real problem. Many younger musicians, very good ones, think of their work as "American classical music."[15] They play what their teachers play, and sometimes what they hear on records. All art forms go through such cycles, when they absorb and consolidate the revolutionary changes of earlier decades; jazz has done this before, although perhaps not in such a thorough way. Although what gets played is often beautiful, it does not convey that thrilling, privileged sense of the best improvised music, that it is saying something that has never been said before. If it is not original, it does not have the "aura" of authenticity, the effect of being in the presence of a work of art that is not a copy.[16]

Bobby Sanabria complains about the "American classical music" theme, partly because it slights the latin influence:

These young guys who want to play traditional—I can't understand it. This music is not classical. This music is about going against the grain. It's revolutionary. It's about saying something new. And so it's also about suffering and paying dues.[17]

Joel Forrester is a pianist who has been in New York twenty years going against the grain, trying to say something new and at the same time to make a living in this city where so many doubt that it can be done. He dismisses using clubs as "showcases;" he is interested in working and getting paid. Years ago, he studied and absorbed the music of Ornette Coleman, as well as the traditional New Orleans music of King Oliver and Jelly Roll Morton. As a result, he found it hard to find other musicians to play with. He now calls himself a "two-fisted pianist"— rooted in the stride tradition, with a strong left hand. He plays only his own compositions. When I heard him play a solo gig at Teddy's in Brooklyn, a handsome, old-fashioned place with a stamped tin ceiling and stained glass transoms over the windows, he played several blues, a tango titled "I Wonder" and a rapid, repetitive piece, not boring but oddly narcotic, that he calls "Industrial Arts." He is the pianist in the Microscopic Septet—three rhythm and four saxophones—for which he writes witty, swinging compositions. His music is unclassifiable, with references to almost every era; at last I am beginning to understand what it means to be "post-modern." The now-defunct weekly *Seven Days* once called the group "the most under-rated band in New York."

Forrester says he now works on three fronts, solo piano and composition, smaller groups like trios and quintets, and writing and playing for the septet. Of the change in the law, he says:

It has helped my pocketbook a lot—helped on all fronts. It used to be more cut and dried in the clubs. The club owners had a certain idea about what was expected. It is better now because we can use a larger band, like the septet, and we can express more ideas.

It has changed the atmosphere. Musicians can exchange more information. At the Manhattan Chili Company, we organised a musicians' cooperative that meets every Tuesday. We have a rotating roster of musicians who can choose the others for a festival of one kind of another. I organized a festival of two-fisted piano—two piano players working separately and together.

It would be great if the union could do more for us—exchange information and help people to get work.[18]

CHAPTER 9

CONCLUSION: POLITICS, LAW AND MUSIC

The situation in which vernacular music, especially jazz, was placed in New York City, as well as the actions taken by the musicians for change in its legal status, have to be understood as the result of several forces. These include the social and economic characteristics of the clubs, popular tastes and social mores about music, the history and politics of the musicians union, the needs of the musicians themselves, conventional zoning policies and finally city government, all operating within a framework of laws, including state and more especially local regulations, procedural rules for administrative agencies and courts, as well as federal labor laws and the Constitution. The laws both shape and are shaped by the other social institutions.

SOCIAL AND POLITICAL PROCESSES

Clubs that offer vernacular music have changed since the time of Prohibition. The clubs have always been sought out by young, middle-class listeners looking for ever more intimate, bohemian hangouts. The few years in the sixties when young people were deserting the bars for coffeehouses with entertainment was a particularly dramatic moment in that search, which has not been abandoned even though the entertainment has largely left the coffeehouses. For the most part, people no longer dance to live music in the clubs, which have also come to be less subject to the control of underworld characters and their allies, perhaps because the clubs are less profitable. For the last forty years, music clubs have had some characteristics in common. They tend to be small, and consequently economically marginal and risky, squeezed by their expenses, particularly by rents. Often, perhaps usually, they grow up out of neighborhood hangouts that begin to offer music to attract a more diverse crowd; they remain stable if their rents permit them to continue.

From the point of view of the musicians, the clubs are places for them to play—to express themselves, to develop their art, and even to get some economic support. The situation of the musicians has much in common with that of all artists, especially in New York City. Like painters, dancers, and other musicians, these artists are commonly underpaid, harassed by rents and looking for places to work, to display their work, and to get support for it. From that point of view, it is not surprising that some clubs take advantage of the situation to pay little or nothing to the performers. Performance arts like music are characteristically social; they come into being before an audience, often performed by a coordinated group. Jazz music intensifies this characteristic when it is improvised, because the music is different each time it is played. A central characteristic of jazz, like other vernacular music, is that it grows from popular roots; it can be and often is played as "entertainment" in urban joints. Thus jazz musicians find all the perennial problems of the American urban artist translated into the boozy, bohemian world of the bar and restaurant.

Despite its popular roots, jazz, like other vernacular music with which it is closely allied, such as rock, has from time to time taken an intensely oppositional stance to commercial music as well as to the standards of middle-class life; at the same time, because it is "entertainment," being played for the profit of the club owner, there is a constant economic push to make the music palatable to a larger group of people. Like the joints where jazz has been played, the music is both part of and a necessary escape from urban life, sometimes in conflict with daytime existence. Other arts of course, may be equally or more oppositional, but they are not so often linked with popular "low-life" resorts.

The role of the musicians union, as the major craft union for a group of artists that had been able to organize everyone in its field, lent a particular cast to the problems of musicians as artists in America. Many musicians, even when they hoped to express themselves as artists without compromise, still expected to be paid at least a craftsman's wages. Mechanical reproduction of music, through records, radio, films, television and even synthesizers, together with changes in laws and public attitudes about organized labor, weakened the union to the point where musicians who do not play commercial music have come to face their economic problems much as other artists, expecting poor pay and hoping through some lucky combination to become famous and in demand.

Like other arts, jazz and popular entertainment generally have provoked a strong impulse to control by the government, one that is easily translated, in the case of live vernacular music, into licensing and zoning policy for the clubs. The cabaret laws were a form of censorship of those arts, as well as of a seductive life that went with them, that were thought to be corrupting. During Prohibition, the regulation of cabarets could be cast as control of speakeasies and the criminals connected with them; after the repeal of Prohibition, the announced policy of regulation changed slightly, toward the attempt to drive "degenerates" out of the business and to limit the corrosive effects of the life identified with the clubs. Administered by the police as a collection of petty rules that invited evasion, the regulation of clubs reproduced the characteristics it was supposed to control by degrading the status of the artists and attracting to the club world "wiseguys" who would know how to run an efficient business while accommodating the rules.

In later years, the regulations were expressed in a *lingua franca* of zoning policy that spoke in terms of crowds, congestion, the hazards of attracting strangers and a decline in the "quality of life." There are of course, traffic problems produced by clubs, even though most jazz clubs are too small to create much congestion; their owners usually wish they could provoke a little more of a traffic problem. The invidious discrimination hidden in the zoning policy—the racism, the contempt for vernacular arts, the fear of what is oppositional or bohemian—is revealed in the failure to take similar action against other uses, like simple bars and restaurants, that have indistinguishable effects.

By the eighties, the City adhered to these policies rather weakly; it had no strong interest in regulating clubs with music only. The regulations, together with the image of the clubs, might have been changed over time if the clubs had been organized to lobby the city administration the way hotels and restaurants have done. The discrimination continued partly because of an ill-defined contempt for vernacular arts, but also because of the inability of the clubs to take concerted action; thus the campaign against the regulation of the clubs fell to the musicians and Local 802.

The smaller club owners have shown scarcely any of the organization that might enable them to advance their interests as a business group. The union, on the other hand, for reasons rooted chiefly in the labor laws, has found it difficult in the last twenty years to "organize" the clubs from a labor point of view. In the years since the Petrillo presidency, the union has tried to use existing law and the courts to strengthen its ability to organize. As it has run up against problems both of delay and unfavorable results, it has turned to lobbying and legislative reform. In the case of the cabaret laws, faced with a situation in which the clubs were not organized in their own interests, and having been unable to organize them in the interests of its members, Local 802 sought legislation to help music indirectly by changing the regulation of clubs.

The union, with a sense that its power was limited, at first handled the political system quite gingerly; with my collaboration as well as that of a lot of other volunteers, including its members, the union sought to eliminate the discrimination among instruments in the exception for "incidental musical entertainment." We started working within the agenda that the law and the political situation set for us; like many organizations, we went after what seemed attainable. That agenda caused us for a short time to confuse what was needed with what was possible.

When that effort failed, the musicians and their union undertook litigation on behalf of the artists rather than the places where they played. Because it was brought against licensing and zoning, however, this litigation at the same time directly affected the clubs. The resulting legal change did not cover all the needs of the clubs; it did nothing for social dancing, and almost nothing for other forms of entertainment like comedy. Having been started by musicians, in the end the change largely helped musicians.

The political system that the union confronted is familiar, and at the same time puzzling. New York City government gives an impression of fragmentation. Day to day regulation is carried out through a number of agencies; in the case of nightclubs, these include City Planning, Consumer Affairs (licensing) and the Fire and Buildings Departments. Thus any restaurant that sought before 1988 to offer more live music than a trio had to have a cabaret license, and any restaurant that sought a cabaret license had to be located in a proper zone before the licensing authorities would act favorably. Correspondingly, any change in the regulations has to affect all the regulatory processes at once in order to be effective. The decision-making process for changes in zoning policy has been still further decentralized, to draw in some "grassroots" influence. Nevertheless, whenever a major decision has to be made, the fragmentation tends to return power to the center, which has the patience, expertise and influence to coordinate all the elements. For people outside the central administration, it is difficult to get the attention of the relevant decision-makers, and even more difficult to get them to make a coordinated decision. When an outside group wants to go beyond the approval for a single project such as a nightclub, or even a building, to reach out for approval of a coordinated change in the legal regulations themselves, the process is dauntingly difficult without the cooperation of City Hall. Thus the sheer complexity of the regulatory and political system becomes a source of power and resistance to change.

In the last thirty years, as the courts have become more hospitable to civil rights cases against state and local regulations, it has come to seem natural to turn to litigation for such change. If a theory is available that cuts across the jurisdiction of the various agencies, as the free expression theory in the cabaret case cut across the licensing and zoning functions, then the case can be used to coordinate change on several fronts. And even if the case is not as successful in the courts as the cabaret case turned out to be, even if it should lead, for example, to a compromised result, nevertheless when the arguments in the case, like the free expression argument against the cabaret laws, have some merit, they serve at least to get the attention of decision-makers, to put the problems of the case on the public agenda.

The assertion of a legal argument that has some merit in the sense that it has to be answered, is thus the assertion of a small amount of power, the power at least to organize and present politically viable arguments and require them to be heard. If those arguments are taken up by the press and the public, as well as by an organization like Local 802, then they take on a life of their own; they have to be dealt with not only through the legal process, but as an independent political organizing force. Thus the cabaret case, combined with the City's increased enforcement in the eighties, served to focus the attention of the press on the cabaret laws, and as the press questioned the City's policies, it became more difficult for the City to adhere to them.

Rights like those asserted in the cabaret case are protean. They can help to emancipate people from regulations that conflict with them, while they tend to imprison us within the terms of the liberty argument. Both effects appeared repeatedly in our effort to change the cabaret laws. It began as an attack on the unfairness of the discrimination against instruments in which exception for "incidental musical entertainment"; as such, it was limited to removing that discrimination. After the argument was refocused as one for the free expression of musicians, it took on new life. The musicians were not very interested in winning a legal argument; they wanted to be able to play where they pleased and as they pleased. In the end, then, we demanded the liberty that was implied by the assertion of freedom of expression for musicians; thus we sought to sweep away the exception for "incidental musical entertainment." But we did not demand that the scope of the liberty be extended further, to comedy, for example, mostly because we did not know how to make the demand without the help of comedians. And we did not find a way to push beyond the First Amendment argument and break through to a basic change in the City's zoning policy.

The acceptance of our demands by the courts was not the end of the political process, as earlier chapters show in detail. The City resisted the legal change, without actually reversing the court decision, for a period of two years; it took a new city administration to put an end to the process.

That resistance and acquiescence, of course, raise the question of what force, what importance ought to be attributed to the assertion of constitutional rights through litigation. Rights, even when asserted successfully, obviously did not bring about change in any simple way. What they did, it seems, was organize and channel thinking about the opportunity for change. They enabled the musicians to think in terms of a greater liberty to play, and thus to make an articulate demand for this liberty. And the resulting case forced the City to confront the demand and take a position on it. There is no question that the presence of a respectable First Amendment argument against the City's zoning and licensing policies was important; without the argument, there was no way to reorganize people's thinking, either that of the musicians or the City. The City's powers of zoning and licensing were nearly unlimited in the absence of the rights arguments. For us to ask for change, through litigation or any other way, without the framework of those arguments was useless; it had no significance and would not have been heard. With the argument, we could expect the support of the press and presentation of the issue in the very favorable terms of resistance to oppression.

THE SIGNIFICANCE OF THE CITY'S RESISTANCE

The account I have just given of the New York City cabaret laws and their change has "naturalized" and domesticated the story. I have been shunting aside still unanswered question that make the persistence of the regulations more of a mystery. Why did New York continue a Prohibition-era system, with only minor changes, that lumped together every sort of entertainment for licensing and zoning purposes, for more than sixty years?

Part of the reason has to be, I believe, that the underlying significance of places of entertainment has not changed very much in those years. They still have the mark of the bohemian; they are places where we drink and let ourselves go. And the music, whether jazz, rock, or some other vernacular form, is represented as music that helps us let ourselves go. It is not represented like the classical arts, as arts of detachment and reason that are observed sober and soberly dressed, from rows of numbered seats. And so such arts give rise to a double reaction: they are on the one hand legitimate subjects of control, and on the other, they are not of such cultural importance that we ought to be concerned about the control that is used against them.

The persistence of these attitudes was reflected in the justifications given for the continued regulation. At first it was the danger of criminality or degeneracy to be found in the joints and in the arts performed in them. The origin of those justifications was racism, in addition to a more unfocused fear of the vernacular. The generalized legal form of the regulations—directed against all "entertainment," as well as more particularly against horns and percussion and larger musical groups—concealed that purpose, ironically spreading the damage of the regulations to all musicians of whatever race, and to all music.

When the argument that the music and its players and patrons were "degenerate" ceased to be respectable, because too baldly discriminatory, the generalized form of the regulations lent itself to a justification about the dangers of congestion, crowds and strangers to the neighborhood. I need not belabor the resemblances between this argument and the original one. They represent powerful unspoken judgments expressing some of society's attitudes about respectability and status as well as race. They certainly are not peculiar to New York. The same terms are used when municipalities limit the outlets for "adult movies" and the like. And it is almost standard to raise fears of "trash" and "congestion" against places of entertainment; the city of Springfield, Massachusetts, for example, recently used them as a way of denying a license to a center for young people that did not sell liquor but competed with existing places in town.[1] The terminology is all about sanitation, betraying how officials think of the world of live entertainment as unclean and disorderly. The attraction of such ideas is powerful; they cannot be answered adequately by mere empirical evidence, but only by another idea that is more commanding, such as an appeal to rights backed by popular support.

Such regulations persist, then, because the views that undergird them do not change; but they persist also because the attitudes become invisible, concealed within the bland generality of legal directives. A bureaucracy—in this case, several bureaucracies, including the City Planning, Consumer Affairs and Fire Departments—is charged with enforcing the directives. City officials learn the rules, part of an even larger pattern of arcane regulations, together with the justifications given for them. Part of their job is to reproduce them by enforcing them, and by explaining them to citizens and to officials who come after them.

I have tried to show that those who gave the justifications for the cabaret regulations believed or at any rate accepted them. Although it seems strange to think that the City's police commissioner could have believed, for example, that there was enough danger from those who played in clubs to justify a system of surveillance, I see no reason to doubt that he accepted the argument. When a state law was passed to eliminate that system in 1959, the City opposed the legislation on the ground, advanced specifically by the Police Commissioner, that its cabarets presented peculiar problems. Similarly, at the present time, the special safety requirements for places of entertainment are justified on the ground that entertainment becomes a "focus of attention" requiring extra safety precautions, even though there is no empirical evidence that there is such a danger. Having performed the accomplishment of learning them, together with their justifications, those who administer the regulations can be expected to reproduce them unless their superiors make a concerted effort to change the rules.

To a lesser extent, those who were subject to the regulations accepted them at least as a given, if not as really justified. When the City stopped effectively enforcing the laws against music-only clubs in the seventies, however, the regulations lost whatever shred of legitimacy they had; that is what led to their demise.

That sequence of events, in turn, makes it puzzling that the City tried to perpetuate or slightly renovate the regulations during the eighties. I offered a bureaucratic-legal explanation in Chapter Five for the City's apparent crackdown on the clubs during the eighties, rooted in increased enforcement powers, together with the end of the municipal fiscal crisis. The infusion of money alone, however, cannot explain the persistence of the system. We have to add that, so long as the form of the regulations remained, the failure to enforce them could be seen as a dereliction of duty.

These words do not solve the puzzle, because the rationales, both overt and implied, for the regulations seem to me to have run very thin by the eighties. This can be illustrated by an ironic event at the end of 1986, after the decision by Justice Saxe eliminating the discrimination among instruments, but while the three-instrument rule prevailed, and the crackdown on larger groups was in full swing. On December 19 of that year the City Council passed a resolution declaring jazz to be a City and a national treasure.[2] In the light of that moment of municipal piety, we can step back and repeat the question of why the City continued its enforcement policy. Some officials undoubtedly did think that New York was the "jazz capital" and did think the music a treasure. Why were they doing their best to suppress it? An easy answer would be that what the City Council puts in a resolution is not necessarily policy; the Department of Consumer Affairs may still want to enforce the law. But I think the answer must lie at a somewhat deeper level, since the City Council had the power to get rid of at least some of the regulations, yet did not try to eliminate the licensing when the resolution was passed.

I believe the explanation must lie in the fact that the City was seeking to retain and extend its control over the entertainment business, without being able to recognize how damaging the system of licensing was. City officials thought that the club business was economically strong, even rich, and could withstand a little regulation. A telltale remark was made by a spokesperson of the Department of Consumer Affairs when she said, "The rationale, I guess, is that the bigger the band, the bigger the place."[3] At some level, they must have thought that an establishment that was important could not be poor. How could a "treasure," after all, be poor?

In his analysis of the drives underlying the City's zoning policy, which I drew on for a sketch of that policy in Chapter Seven, Paul Goldberger goes beyond the push for regulation and economic development to find an "imperial" drive—toward making New York City more powerful and dominant as well as richer.[4] That impulse was at work in the eighties; regulatory systems favored the strong. The system of bargaining for the privilege of running a club or other land-use actions in the City only strengthened the effect. Those who had great resources could bargain with the City, give the municipality something while still getting most of what they wanted. Those who had few resources could not bargain at all. The plan proposed by City Planning at the very end, for licensing clubs by special permit, was calculated to favor chiefly those with considerable staying power. Thus the City sought to extend its control deeper into the life of the city at the expense of those who could not withstand the system of regulation.

The theory advanced by some musicians, like Bob Belden, that the City's crackdown on the clubs was linked to "gentrification" or "real estate interests," has some truth to it, then. All the City's policies, including those relating to commercial rents, were pushing toward more expensive, "imperial" commercial uses.

Yet the process came to a stop, partly because of a change in administration, and partly because the frenzied inflation in real estate values had come to an end. Does the City's abandonment of its policies of sixty years, rooted as they were in an unspoken sense that the vernacular arts were neither respectable nor important, mean that the City has, at some level, recognized those arts as respectable? Without making too much of the point, I think it has. The rhetoric of our argument against the regulations for music clubs pointed chiefly to the example of jazz, which has largely become accepted. Some of those who play it, as well as some listeners, think of it as "American classical music," if not as something even more ordinary—just "something with a mood to it," as the woman in the Brooklyn club said. Acceptance by the City may mean that the music is perceived as having lost its cutting edge of resistance.

If that is true, then history tells us that the lull is a passing phase. In the twentieth century, the vernacular arts have always appealed to the rebels, among both listeners and performers. Jazz still shows its cutting edge, in smaller places and among musicians, some of them older people still identified with the avant-garde. And insofar as that edge has been dulled, it will either sharpen again, or the music will be so transformed by other influences as to become unrecognizable, and will show its edge in another form. The City, after all, has not done the musicians such a great favor in changing the zoning and licensing regulations; all it has done is make it possible to create places to play the music. Those places still have to come into being, and the musicians still have to work in them in order to learn the art and be heard by listeners. The musicians still confront the problems of poor pay and difficult working conditions.

MUSIC AND AUTONOMY

Reading over this analysis leads me to ask a last question. What does the vitality of the music mean for us? If we have any faith that the music will, from time to time, work itself free of commercial demands or turn them to its own purposes, that it will exhibit some autonomy, should we have a similar hope about law? We have very different expectations about law, it seems, but what is the justification for them?

We don't expect law to have the same sort of social independence as art, at least in the modern world where it has become basic to the function—almost to the definition—of art that it be removed from the practical problems and demands of everyday life. Under contemporary circumstances, moreover, expressing something different from what was said before has become essential for an artist to be seen or heard.[5] Law, on the other hand, is based in norms that have political roots, bound around under modern conditions with bureaucratic regulation, so that, most of the time, we expect and even hope that the legal system will say something predictable rather than something unpredictable. And yet we react to legal phenomena as though they are autonomous, as though their structures not only can be relied on to produce predictable results, but can be changed to produce different ones.

We ought to understand institutional autonomy in at least two different ways, one implicating continuity and the other implicating change. In one sense, law is autonomous just insofar as it does not respond to demands for change from outside the legal system. That sort of autonomy is essential to law, and this book is shot through with examples of it. The federal labor laws have taken a form for at least the last forty years that has made the organization of the musicians union difficult; yet the courts have adhered to their interpretation of those laws until there seems to be no solution except a return to Congress for more amendments. The demand for decentralization of land-use planning in New York led, some fifteen years ago, to a statutory framework in which it is extremely difficult to change zoning policy. The City cabaret-licensing and zoning system itself was established more than sixty years ago, and continued basically unchanged until virtually yesterday. To be sure, these frameworks of law are rooted in social and political decisions that are outside them. The Taft-Hartley amendments to the federal labor laws were supposed to make organizing a union, at least one like the musicians union, more difficult; the changes in New York City land-use planning were supposed to decentralize decisions about zoning; the cabaret-licensing system was based on an invidious view of vernacular music and dance as well as of nightlife generally. Yet the frameworks have an institutional life of their own. They are enduring because bureaucracies are established that understand and administer them, and have an interest in their continuation. It is this sort of regularity that Weber[6] and much of the European tradition has understood as the autonomy of law.

This aspect of autonomy works a little like a style or tradition in the arts, jealously guarded by conservatives who will insist that students learn and use accepted means of expression. It creates such a strong sense of what is acceptable that when traditional critics encounter rebellious expression, they typically react by saying that it "isn't music" or "isn't art." It is this sort of received view, which shows its social power by its command of funds and public acceptance, from which modern artists, including musicians, have been in flight for generations, although contemporary "post-modern" feelings are a little more ambiguous. Traditionalism in art has been under attack so systematically that we can scarcely conceive of it as a form of "autonomy" at all. Institutional autonomy of the sort that seems at the heart of law is thus largely denigrated in the arts; it is the autonomy of the artist or his group to depart from the received and expected that is honored. It has been the historic function of progressive artists to recognise how institutionalized forms and modes of expression reflect the control of other forces in society, and then to try to devise expressive ways to escape from them. This sort of autonomy freely to search for new modes of expression is supported and fueled by the modern background expectation that art should in any case be free of direct instrumental demands for political and social conformity.

Some American lawyers search for such a Promethean sense of autonomy in the discourse of rights, seeking to organize them creatively through litigation. It is true that some general principles in the Constitution, like free expression, the right of privacy or equal protection of the laws, do express broad and powerful emancipatory aims. And sometimes, as in the first desegregation decisions or the original abortion decision, the courts do use these principles to reorganise social relations in new ways. But when lawyers frame and bring such cases, they do so predicting that change is available within a narrow range of possibilities, rooted in social circumstances and past decisions. As Bourdieu says, "Given the determinant role it plays in social reproduction, the juridical field has a smaller degree of autonomy than other fields, like the artistic or literacy or even the scientific fields, that also contribute to the maintenance of the symbolic order and, thereby, to that of the social order itself."[7]

Rights are themselves part of an institutional framework, that can be put into dialogue with other parts of the legal system. The business of change through litigation is one of trying to understand social forces, even to channel them through legal discourse, and to use the institutions of the legal system to reflect them.

A critic like Foucault[8] might well say that an "autonomous" creative act by an artist is not very different, because its autonomy is in part illusory, enclosed within the framework of knowledge, the institutional framework that is expression. I don't want to reject or embrace that idea here, but instead to say more simply that the experience of the act is very different; the "creative" act is projected to say something that has not been heard before, or show something that has not been seen before. The "rights" act is projected to say something that has been heard before, but to give it an authority that it has not previously had. The legal change represents and reflects, in symbolic terms, a change in society: although it may also help to bring about change, it can do so only within an institutional framework of law prepared to accept the change as part of a larger tradition.

Chart of New York City Cabaret Licensing and Zoning 1916–1990

Year	Zoning	Licensing
1916	NYC begins land-use planning.	
1926	Nightclubs restricted in zoning.	"cabaret" licensing of nightclubs begins.
1931		Police assume licensing functions.
1940		Identity cards for entertainers begin.
1955	Change in definition of cabaret to permit "incidental musical entertainment" by a trio (only keyboards and strings) in zones where cabarets forbidden.	
1961	Present form of Zoning Resolution adopted; cabaret zones restricted.	Cabaret licensing transferred to Dept. of Licenses; "incidental musical entertainment" permitted in unlicensed clubs.
1967		Identity cards abolished.
1971		One singer permitted as part of "incidental musical entertainment."
1983		Messinger bill proposes to change "incidental musical entertainment" to permit any sort of instruments.
1986	Court enjoins, then City Council changes, discrimination against instruments in definition of "incidental musical entertainment" (leaving a law permitting up to three musicians in unlicensed clubs).	
1988	Court declares three-musician rule unconstitutional.	
	NYC Planning Dept. begins drafting new zoning for clubs.	
1990	NYC Planning Dept. accepts a rule permitting live music in zones where bars and restaurants permitted.	

NOTE ON SOURCES

One aspect of this book has been a history of prejudices, shared by municipal elites and politicians, concerning the vernacular arts. Such prejudices are often unspoken, having the effect of marginalizing entertainment by not taking it seriously—"zoning" it into the periphery both literally and figuratively. Until recent years, scholarly works about the arts and even about urban life have tended to share the prejudices, thus marginalizing studies about the popular arts. As this note will demonstrate, there is often little written about issues of importance to this book. What is written is sometimes anecdote, although the anecdotes can be revealing and useful.

As a consequence, this book has turned out to be something of an "underground" research project. A glance at the footnotes will show that I have largely relied on interviews, my own documentary records and sometimes my own recollections. Documents cited in the notes from lawsuits that do not refer to the systematic law reports—that is, materials not contained in published court opinions—are all drawn from cases brought in New York County. The records can be found in the office of the County Clerk of New York County.

Because secondary sources directly covering the story are so few, and because so much of the argument in this book depends on press and public opinion, I have also relied heavily on newspaper sources. I draw upon the daily papers, the *New York Times*, which is referred to in the notes by the shorthand "NYT," as well as the *Daily News*, the *New York Post*, and New York

Newsday. I am grateful to all of their able journalists who report the local scene and its music. In addition, I have drawn on the weekly papers, the *Village Voice* and the *Amsterdam News*, as well as on the music magazine *Downbeat.*

For Chapter Two, concerned with the history and problems of the American Federation of Musicians, and especially New York's Local 802, I have drawn on the files of the union. Public Relations Director Judy West searched for records that I could not otherwise find. The newspaper of Local 802, *Allegro*, has been cited extensively.

There are three excellent articles that relate the history of the AFM to its legal problems. Two of them are by Vern Countryman, "The Organized Musicians: I" 16 University of Chicago Law Review 56 (1948) and "The Organized Musicians: II" 16 University of Chicago Law Review 239 (1949). These two appear to have been written, at a time when union president James Petrillo was under heavy fire in the popular press, as a way to understand the union's tactics in the light of its history. Robert Gorman, "The Recording Musician and Union Power: A Case Study of the American Federation of Musicians" 37 Southwestern Law Journal 697 (1983), derived from a study conducted by Mr. Gorman for the U.S. Copyright Office, is focussed on the musicians' problems concerning their rights (or the lack of them) to royalties from performances, in the light of the history of the union. The general problem of the distinction between an employee and an independent contractor, as it appears throughout labor relations in the United States, is exhaustively surveyed in Marc Linder, *The Employment Relationship in American Law* (Westport: Greenwood Press, 1989).

For Chapters Three and Four, concerned with the history of the clubs in the New York City and the sixty-year history of the cabaret laws, I drew on several archives. In the Theater and Music Collections of the New York Public Library at Lincoln Center, there are files of clippings and other documents concerning the cabaret laws, as well as particular artists and particular clubs, extending back to about 1930.

The Institute for Jazz Studies, at Rutgers University, Newark, New Jersey, has an enormous collection of books, recordings, and memorabilia. It has a file on "cabaret cards," which appears to be largely material collected by the late George Hoefer, a jazz aficionado and columnist for *Downbeat*. This file contains typescripts by Hoefer, apparently drafts of writings intended for *Downbeat*, concerning the cabaret cards in the fifties and sixties. I refer to these in the notes as "Hoefer ms." with the dates that appear on the typescripts.

Works on the general history of jazz tend understandably to give little space to descriptions of the places where it was played, at least in New York. Leonard Kunstadt and Samuel Charters, *Jazz: A History of the New York Scene*, (New York: Doubleday, 1962), the standard work on the history of jazz in the City as it was shortly before the book itself was published, contains valuable material on the musicians, and many useful details about the places where they played. There is further material in works on the lives of individual musicians, upon which I have drawn in the notes to Chapters Three and Four. I found particularly useful Eddie Condon, *We Called It Music* (New York: Holt, 1947), which discusses clubs both in Harlem and Midtown Manhattan; A.B. Spellman, *Four Lives in the Bebop Business* (New York: Pantheon Press, 1966), which discusses the Five Spot and other places; Ross Russell, *Bird Lives* (New York: Charterhouse, 1973), which depicts the bebop world both in Harlem and further downtown. There is a myriad of other books that might have been used, without, I believe, changing the picture.

Books centering on the clubs are very few. Perhaps the best is Lewis Erenberg, *Steppin' Out: New York Nightlife and the Transformation of American Culture* (Chicago: University of Chicago 1981). Although its account stops as of 1930 and it is only tangentially related to the music, it is one of the very few books that takes a category such as "nightlife" seriously as a social phenomenon. Arnold Shaw's *52nd Street: The Street of Jazz* (New York: DaCapo, 1977) (republication of *The Street That Never Slept*), seems to be much the best book about a specific group of clubs. Although it employs some *Variety*-style prose, it is essentially a serious historical memoir. Of the many books on Harlem, the one that seems to contain the best account of the jazz clubs is Jervis Anderson, *This Was Harlem: A Cultural Portrait* (NY: Farrar, Straus and Giroux, 1982). There are useful chapters on Harlem nightlife as of the time of publication of the book in J.H. Clarke, *Harlem: A Community in Transition* (New York: Citadel, 1964). The most authoritative piece on the Harlem clubs is George Hoefer's booklet of notes to the set of reissued records, *Jazz Odyssey, Vol. III, Sounds of Harlem,* Columbia C3L33 (1964). There is a copy at the Institute of Jazz Studies, Rutgers University, Newark NJ.

There is more material on the culture of jazz, as distinguished from the places where it was played. The books cited above on the lives of musicians are useful, as are two other books, Whitney Balliett, *Improvising: Sixteen Jazz Musicians and their Art* (New York: Oxford, 1977) and Nat Hentoff, *The Jazz Life* (New York: Da Capo, 1975). Much of the material scattered in other books is collected and analyzed in the anthropological study by Neil Leonard, *Jazz: Myth and Religion* (New York: Oxford, 1987). Although by the standards of most jazz writing this sort of study is "academic," it is insightful and illuminating.

The attitudes of the jazz audience are also studied in Neil Leonard's book just cited. His earlier book, *Jazz and the White Americans* (Chicago: University of Chicago, 1962) is the best thing written about changing social attitudes to the music. The demographic composition of the contemporary jazz audience is surveyed in H. Horowitz, "American Jazz Audience" (Washington, D.C.: National Jazz Service Organization, mimeo, 1986). The appropriation by painters and other modern artists of inprovisatory and other methods from jazz is reflected in T. Gioia, *The Imperfect Art: Reflections on Jazz and Modern Culture* (New York: Oxford, 1988). I have used Walter Benjamin,'s "The Work of Art in the Age of Mechanical Reproduction," in *Illuminations* (New York: Schocken, 1969) as a source for a general framework for talking about the irreplaceable originality of an art that is performed live, including the "aura" that surrounds something genuinely "original," in the sense both of a unique object and an original creation.

The materials I have used for the arguments concerning land-use and zoning in Chapters Five and Seven are quite diverse. My criticism of prejudices implicit in New York City zoning policy is drawn from a systematic lack, as much as it is from arguments directly made in the literature. For example, standard works on planning such as Mel Scott, *American City Planning since 1890* (Berkeley and Los Angeles: University of California Press, 1969) or F. S. Chapin Jr. and E. J. Kaiser, *Urban Land Use Planning* (Urbana: University of Illinois Press, 1979) do not mention night-time places of resort at all. It is the long-standing attempt to imagine and create a "planned" environment that has led to this situation in the literature, as is implied in Christine Boyer, *Dreaming the Rational City: The Myth of American City Planning* (Cambridge, MA: MIT Press, 1983). A seminal work that critiques the tradition, Jane Jacobs, *Death and Life of Great American Cities* (New York: Random House, 1961), while it speaks in terms of local neighborhood activities, unplanned and vital, is focussed largely on daytime activities helpful to families, such as those of strollers and storekeepers. Richard Sennett, *The Fall of Public Man* (New York: Vintage, 1978) directly critiques the moral repressiveness of much urban planning. Ray Oldenburg, *The Great Good Place* (New York: Paragon House, 1989), is an idiosyncratic work of sociology that, in championing evening watering-places, points out how land-use theory has failed to account for them.

The contrast drawn in Chapter Five between a controlled-community and an urban-diversity ideal of urban life is based in part on Jane Jacobs, *op.cit.*, and more directly on William H. Whyte, *The City: Rediscovering the Center* (New York: Doubleday, 1988). I have drawn some analogies from the study of suburbs, which are viewed as intensely controlled environments in M.P. Baumgartner, *The Moral Order of a Suburb* (New York: Oxford, 1988) and in Sally Merry's analysis of the town of

Wellesley, MA., "Mending Walls and Building Fences" (presented at the meeting of the Law and Society Association, June, 1990). These describe societies made up of private homes, islands of safety isolated from one another. A much more sympathetic view is Herbert Gans, *The Levittowners* (New York: Pantheon Press, 1967). The difference lies partly, I think, in the age and class of the residents. The Levittowners were lower middle class young people with young children. It seems reasonable to conclude that interdependent action was more necessary and congenial to them than it would be to the older and more wealthy residents of the suburbs described by Merry and Baumgartner. As I point out in the book, however, I do not see that the characteristics of either group are restricted to suburbs.

The critique of New York's incentive zoning policies is drawn from W.H. Whyte, *op. cit.*, as well as from Richard Sennett, *op. cit.* and from a crisp statement of the problem in a report published by the Natural Resources Defense Council and the Womens City Club, "New York City Zoning: The Need for Reform" (1989). The costs of earlier policies are succinctly analyzed in Jerold Kayden, *Incentive Zoning in New York City: A Cost-Benefit Analysis* (Lincoln Inst. of Land Policy, 1978). A discussion of recent city land policy is Paul Goldberger, "Shaping the Face of New York," in Peter Salins, ed., *New York Unbound* (New York: Blackwell, 1988), pp. 127–140. A similar discussion appears in H.V. Savitch, *Post-Industrial Cities: Politics and Planning in New York, Paris and London* (Princeton: Princeton University, 1988).

NOTES

Notes to Introduction

1. E. Samler, "If Jazz Quartet's on Stage, Lawyer Can Take a Bow," NYT, April 24, 1988, p. A42.

2. In Ronald Dworkin's writings, of course, the judge is cast as the hero (often actually called "Hercules"), and the principles of law are viewed as sufficiently general and flexible to afford plenty of room for heroic feats of insight toward interpretation. In this view, nevertheless, rights are strongly autonomous; there is a correct view toward which decision-making "works itself pure." R. Dworkin, *Law's Empire* (Cambridge, MA: Harvard University 1986) pp. 400–410.

3. See, e.g., B. Selcraig, "Reverend Wildmon's War on the Arts," NYT Magazine, September 2, 1990, p. 22.

4. J. Gusfield, "On Legislating Morals: The Symbolic Process of Designating Deviancy," 56 California Law Review 54, 58 (1968).

5. The mayors mentioned in later chapters, with their terms of office, are Robert Wagner, 1954 to 65; John Lindsay, 1966 to 73; Abraham Beame, 1974 to 77; Edward Koch, 1978 to 1989; and the incumbent, David Dinkins, who took office in 1990.

6. *Board of Estimate v. Morris*, 489 U.S. 688 (1989).

Notes to Chapter 1

1. Affidavit of Monica Hughes, May 9, 1986, in *Chiasson, et al. v. NYC Dept of Consumer Affairs et al.*, Supreme Court, New York County Index No. 11839/86 (hereafter "*Chiasson* record").

2. NYC Administrative Code section B32-296.0 (1971) (later recodified as section 20-359).

3. "Incidental musical entertainment" was defined in NYC Zoning Resolution, sections 32-15A; 73-242; 73-243 (1961). Commercial districts zoned to permit an application for a cabaret license, so that more than incidental musical

entertainment could be offered in a bar or restaurant, were designated C4 (major commercial centers); C6 (high-bulk commercial); C7 (amusement parks); C8 (commercial-industrial) and manufacturing districts (M). In certain other commercial districts, it was possible to get a special permit from the Board of Standards and Appeals. *Zoning Resolution* section 73-241. This system is described in more detail in Chapters Five and Seven.

4. Conversation with Sonny Fortune, June 11, 1990.

5. G. Goodman, "Jazz Combo Sounds Protest Note on Cabaret Law," NYT March 5, 1985, p. C15; Editorial "Free the Fipple Flute," Daily News, March 8, 1985, p. 33; Cartoon, Daily News, March 6, 1985.

6. J. Pareles, "City Forces Clubs to Restrict Jazz," NYT April 10, 1986, p. C13.

7. See, for example, the description of litigation against police Red Squads in P. Chevigny, "Politics and Law in the Control of Local Surveillance," 69 Cornell Law Review 735 (1984).

8. Affidavit of Warren Chiasson, May 23, 1986, *Chiasson* record.

9. Affidavit of Mark Morganelli, May 21, 1986, *Chiasson* record.

Notes to Chapter 2

1. V. Countryman, "The Organized Musicians: I," 16 University of Chicago Law Review 56, 57 (1948) (hereafter "Countryman I").

2. Constitution and By-laws, Local 802, AFM, Article IV section 1gg (1988).

3. Between 1929 and 1931, the number of musicians performing in motion picture theaters declined from 22000 to 5000. R. Gorman, "The Recording Musician and Union Power: A Case Study of the American Federation of Musicians," 37 South Western Law Journal 697, 700 (1983) (hereafter "Gorman").

4. It is a peculiarity of the copyright law that while composers are entitled to royalties when their compositions are broadcast, musical performers are not entitled to royalties for performances of their recordings, 17 USCA section 114; *RCA Mfg. Co. v. Whiteman,* 114 F.2d 86 (2 Cir. 1940) cert. den. 311 U.S. 712 (1940), discussed in Gorman at 704. Thus the musicians did not have to be paid royalties on the broadcast of recordings that would displace them. It is worth noting that all this was slightly beside the point for Petrillo; he was less interested in royalties for a few recording musicians than in continued employment for live musicians. Gorman 705–728; V. Countryman, "The Organized Musicians: II" 16 University of Chicago Law Review 239 (1949).

5. The Lea Act, 60 Stat. 89 (1946), was repealed by 94 Stat. 2747 (1980). The Taft-Hartley provisions are 29 USC section 158 (b)(4); (6) and section 186. Gorman at 722–28. The ban on recordings, as a means of putting pressure on broadcasters, for example, was arguably a "secondary boycott."

6. Gorman at 783.

7. Countryman I at 71.

8. For Parker, Russell, Ross, *Bird Lives* (New York: Charterhouse, 1973) p. 102. For the New Gardens, Kunstadt, L. and Charters, S. *Jazz: A History of the New York Scene* (New York: Doubleday, 1962) p. 355.

9. Countryman I pp. 71–2.

10. *Ibid.*, 70–71.

11. For Sammy Sands, S. Schmidt, "Now, a Robot at the Piano," NYT July 27, 1984, II:8; for synthesizers, "Radio City Threatens Lockout; Christmas Show May Utilize Synthetic Music," *Allegro* September 1990, p. 1.

12. 29 USC section 158(a)(3).

13. Under its policy of legislative lobbying, Local 802 persuaded the New York legislature in 1989 to adopt a law permitting the period to be shortened to seven days under agreements in the performing arts. NYS Labor Law, 30 *McKinney's Consol. Laws of NY,* section 704-a (1989). Its effect is not yet clear.

14. In *AFM v. Carroll,* 391 US 99 (1968), the Supreme Court ruled that it was legally permissible for the union to establish "price floors" for the club date bandleaders to pass on to their customers.

15. J. Rogers, "Divide and Conquer: Further 'Reflections on the Distinctive Character of American Labor Laws' " 1990 Wisconsin Law Review 1, 54.

16. *NLRB v. MacKay Radio & T. Co.,* 304 US 333 (1938); *TWA v. Intern. Fed of Flight Attendants,* 489 US 426 (1989).

17. R. Samborn, " 'Replacements' Spur Labor Action" *National Law Journal,* May 28, 1990, p. 1.

18. *Allen-Bradley Co. v. IBEW,* 352 U.S. 797 (1945).

19. *NLRB v. Hearst Pub. Inc.,* 322 US 111, 126–7 (1944).

20. 29 USC section 152 (3); Senator Taft, 93 Congressional Record 6441–42.

21. Restatement of the Law of Agency 2d (St. Paul, ALI 1958) section 220.

22. Linder, M. *Employment Relationship in Anglo-American Law* (Westport: Greenwood, 1989) p. 201.

23. *Local 777, Dem. Union Org. Comm. v. NLRB,* 603 F.2d 862, 906 (D.C. Cir. 1978).

24. *Hilton Intern. Co. v. NLRB,* 690 F.2d 318 (2d Cir. 1982); Morris, Charles, ed. *Developing Labor Law* (DC: Bureau of Nat'l Affairs 1983) Vol. II pp. 1464–1488.

25. Conversation with John Glasel, May 14, 1990.

26. Conversation with Milton Hinton, June 17, 1990. Within the confines of jazz, white musicians have also complained about discrimination by black musicians.

27. Affidavit of John Glasel, May 1, 1986, *Chiasson* record.

28. Conversation with Peter Sims, June 6, 1990; with John Carisi, Sept. 12, 1990.

29. For the proposed Performing Artists Labor Relations Amendments, see, e.g., *Allegro* July/August 1990, p. 5; for New York labor law amendments, NYS Labor Law section 704-a, *supra* note 13.

30. Conversation with David Sheldon, May 10, 1990.

31. In April 1990, when a bandleader was disciplined for working for an employer declared unfair, the bandleader simply resigned from the union. *Allegro*, June 1990, p. 21.

32. *Allegro* April 1990 p. 3; M. Moschel, "The NLRB and Musicians: a Poor Fit," *Allegro* July/August 1990, p. 10. As of this writing, the regional director of the NLRB held that employees of Greene Street were independent contractors, and the union appealed. *Allegro* December 1990, p. 1.

33. Conversation with David Sheldon, May 10, 1990; with Joel Forrester, May 23, 1990.

Notes to Chapter 3

1. Shaw, Arnold, *52nd Street: The Street of Jazz* (New York: DaCapo, 1977) (originally, *The Street That Never Slept*) p. x (hereafter "Shaw").

2. Lena Horne quoted in Anderson, Jervis, *This Was Harlem: A Cultural Portrait* (New York: Farrar, Straus, 1982) p. 175; for Jungle Alley, p. 169 (hereafter "Anderson").

3. Condon, Eddie, *We Called It Music* (New York: 1947) pp. 181–2, 186–91 (hereafter "Condon"); Anderson, p. 170; Ostransky, L., *Jazz City* (Englewood Cliffs: Prentice-Hall, 1978), pp. 200–201.

4. Early comments on jazz are collected in Leonard, Neil, *Jazz and the White Americans* (Chicago: University of Chicago Press, 1970); see also Chapter Five, *infra*.

5. Shaw, pp. 280–81; Russell, Ross, *Bird Lives* (New York: Charterhouse, 1973) p. 163 (hereafter "Russell").

6. Shaw, pp. xii, 63, 263, 318.

7. Shaw, p. 62, 203.

8. Shaw, p. 105; Condon, p. 240.

9. Shaw, p. 117.

10. Shaw, pp. 54, 137, 227, 269, 283, 318.

11. See, e.g. Spellman, A.B., *Four Lives in the Bebop Business* (New York: Pantheon, 1966) (hereafter "Spellman").

12. Condon, p. 182; Shaw, p. 64.

13. Anderson, pp. 347–50; W. Dixon, "Music of Harlem," in Clarke, J.H., *Harlem, A Community in Transition* (New York: Citadel, 1964) pp. 65–75.

14. Russell, pp. 130–144.

15. Spellman, p. 193.

16. Shaw, p. 159.

17. Shaw, p. 252, 268.

18. Russell, p. 164; Shaw, pp. x, 161.

19. Condon, p. 294.

20. Sometime in the early fifties, Ed Allen played at the Central Plaza in a reconstruction of the Clarence Williams band of the twenties, with Buster

Bailey, clarinet, Cyrus St. Clair, tuba, and Baby Dodds, drums. I cannot remember who took Williams' place at the piano. On that occasion, one could hear more clearly what Allen still had to say. See also Chapter Two, note 8.

21. Feather, Leonard, *Encyclopedia of Jazz* (New York: Horizon, 1955) p. 30; Shaw, p. 272.

22. Stearns, Marshall and Jean, *Jazz Dance* (New York: Schirmer, 1979) p. 1.

23. G. Giddins, "The Five Spot Closes. Highs and Lows of a Great Jazz Club," *Village Voice* February 16, 1976, p. 16; conversation with Mike Cantarino, May 14, 1990; J.S. Wilson, "For Half Note Club, It's Midtown Tempo," NYT, Jan. 8, 1974, p. 24.

24. See, e.g., Gioia, T., *The Imperfect Art: Reflections on Jazz and Modern Culture* (New York: Oxford, 1988); Leonard, Neil, *Jazz: Myth and Religion* (New York: Oxford, 1987).

25. Conversation with Joseph Termini, May 20, 1990.

26. Benjamin, Walter, "The Work of Art in the Age of Mechanical Reproduction" in *Illuminations* (New York: Schocken, 1969) pp. 217–251.

27. G. Giddins, *op. cit.*; conversation with Mike Cantarino, May 14, 1990. Cecil Taylor did not find the Terminis nearly as appreciative as he would have liked; Spellman, Chapter One. Nevertheless, hardly any other club hired Taylor's group at that time.

28. J. Wilson, "Cabaret Business Nears Low Point," NYT, March 12, 1964, p. 40. cf. J. Wilson, "Comeback for the Old-Fashioned Nightclubs," NYT, Jan. 27, 1984, p. c1.

29. M. Gansberg, "15 'Village' Shops Ordered to Close," NYT, March 25, 1964, p. 43. See also the account in Chapter Four, *infra*.

30. The most complete account of this period in the Harlem jazz clubs appears to be George Hoefer's booklet of notes to *Jazz Odyssey, Vol. III, Sounds of Harlem*, Columbia Records, C3L33 (1964). There he lists some twelve clubs that had some music in 1964. For Small's Paradise in this period, see J. Williams, "Harlem Nightclub," in Clarke, J.H. *op. cit.* For the audience, H. Horowitz, "American Jazz Audience" (Washington D.C.: National Jazz Svce. Org., mimeo, 1986).

31. See also L. Ledbetter, "Aficionados of Innovative Jazz Get Their Fill at Studio Rivbea" NYT, July 10, 1974, p. 46.

Notes to Chapter 4

1. Erenberg, Lewis, *Steppin' Out: New York Nightlife and the Transformation of American Culture* (Chicago: University of Chicago, 1981) Chapter 1; Shaw, Arnold, *52nd Street: The Street of Jazz* (New York: DaCapo, 1977) p. 12.

2. Erenberg, pp. 114, 135, 141–2.

3. *Ibid.*, pp. 123–4.

4. W. Carr, "The Cabaret Cards and the Cops," *New York Post* November 25, 1960, p. 50.

5. Proceedings of Board of Alderman, City of New York, Dec. 7, 1926, p. 572.

6. *Ibid.*, p. 573.

7. *Ibid.*, p. 574; W. Carr, *op. cit.*, note 5.

8. Leonard, Neal, *Jazz and the White Americans* (Chicago: University of Chicago Press, 1962) pp. 35–38.

9. Quoted in Ullman, Michael, *Jazz Lives* (Washington DC: New Republic, 1980) p. 32.

10. *Matter of Friedman v. Valentine* 30 NYS 2d 891, 894 (Sup. Ct. NY Co. 1941) aff'd 42 NYS 2d 593 (1 Dept. 1943); Alcoholic Beverage Control Law, 3 *McKinney's Consol. Laws of NY* section 102.

11. Material on Billie Holiday from White, J., *Billie Holiday, Her Life and Times* (New York: Universe, 1987) pp. 91–94.

12. Quoted in Hoefer ms, Dec. 22, 1960, p. 7.

13. *Ibid.*, Jan. 19, 1961, pp. 10–11.

14. Quoted in Ullman, *op. cit.*, pp. 33.

15. For Stitt, Hoefer ms, Jan. 5, 1961, p. 7; for Powell, Ullman, *op. cit.*, "Maxwell Cohen," pp. 27–36.

16. Fitterling, T., *Thelonious Monk* (Berlin: Orcos, 1987), p. 62; conversation with Buell Neidlinger, June 27, 1990.

17. Hoefer ms, December 22, 1960, p. 1.

18. *Downbeat* June 25, 1959, p. 9; "Court Test Opens on Cabaret Cards," NYT, May 14, 1959, p. 35; "Trombonist Wins, Gets Cabaret Card," NYT, May 15, 1959, p. 24; Hoefer ms, December 22, 1960, p. 12; January 5, 1961, p. 7.

19. Public Papers of Governor Rockefeller—1959 (Albany: New York State, 1959) p. 272; *Allegro*, February 1959, p. 6; December 1960, p. 1.

20. "The Cabaret Cards—Have They Killed a Man?" *Downbeat*, December 22, 1960; Hoefer ms, December 12, 1960, pp. 1, 11; conversation with Joseph Termini, May 20, 1990.

21. G. Giddins, "The Five Spot Closes. Highs and Lows of a Great Jazz Club," *Village Voice*, February 16, 1976, p. 16.

22. Hoefer ms, December 22, 1960, p. 9.

23. The *New York Times* stories, all from 1960, are: A. Gelb, "Charges of Police Corruption Made by Citizens' Group Here," November 14, p. 1; A. Gelb, "City Will Study Cabaret Charges," November 15, p. 1; A. Gelb, "Inquiry on Police Weighed by State" November 16, p. 1; L. Robinson, "City to Bid Sinatra Testify on Cabarets," November 17, p. 1; L. Robinson, "Rockefeller Asks Report on Cabaret Inquiry Here," November 18, p. 1; G. Passant, "Police Widening Cabaret Inquiry," November 19, p. 1; N. Robertson, "1,000 Policemen Check Cabarets," November 21, p. 1; E. Perlmutter, "Nightclub Losing Permit for 4 Days" November 22, p. 1; E. Perlmutter, "City Lifts Permits of 20 Night Spots," November 23, p. 1; I. Freeman,

"Mayor May Ease Nightclub Rules," November 25, p. 1; I. Freeman, "2 More Cabarets Win Penalty Stage," November 26, p. 23; I. Freeman, "Nightspots Hit by Police Again," November 27, p. 71; E. Perlmutter, "Mayor to Relax Cabaret Rules," November 29, p. 1.

24. E. Perlmutter, "Police to Step Up Vigil on Cabarets," NYT, November 20, 1960, p. 32.

25. Hoefer ms, January 5, 1961, p. 5.

26. J. Sibley, "Police Licensing of Clubs to End," NYT, January 17, 1961, p. 1.

27. *Simone v. Kennedy* 212 NYS 2d 838 (Sup. Ct. NY Co. 1961); see note 9, *supra,* for waiter's union case.

28. Editorial, "Cabaret Card Tempest," NYT, November 29, 1960, p. 36.

29. "Civic Group Backs Cabaret Card Plan," NYT, December 12, 1960, p. 37.

30. P. Benjamin, "City is Criticised on Cafe Licensing," NYT, May 10, 1961, p. 32.

31. Spellman, A.B. *Four Lives in the Bebop Business* (New York: Pantheon 1966) p. 22. Remaining information from conversation with Buell Neidlinger, June 27, 1990; liner notes to Krystall Klear and the Buells, *Ready for the Nineties* K2B2 record No. 2069 (Los Angeles, 1980); *Complete Candid Recordings of Cecil Taylor and Buell Neidlinger* Mosaic Records (Stamford, Conn. 1989).

32. S. Zion, "Mayor Backs End to Cabaret Law," NYT, January 20, 1966, p. 24.

33. The foregoing paragraph draws on the following material from the *New York TImes* for 1966: W. Lissner, "Fingerprinting Rule in Cabarets to End," August 29, p. 1; Editorial, "Two Small Victories," August 30, p. 40. And for 1967: C. Bennett, "Cabaret Staffs Get Mayor's Aid," August 9, p. 4. E. Perlmutter, "Cabaret Card use Ended by Council," September 13, p. 31; "City Urged to Ease Its Licensing Requirements," November 5, p. 118.

34. NYS Alcoholic Beverage Control Law, 3 *McKinney's Consol. Laws of NY* section 102. Under present section 752 of the New York Correction Law, 10B *McKinney's Consol. Laws of NY*, a criminal record may not be used as a bar to licensing unless there is a "direct relationship" between the offense and the license, or an "unreasonable risk" to the public. While the city police regulations phased out in 1966 would probably fail under the latter test, the relation between the two statutes is unresolved.

As a matter of federal Constitutional law, it is well-settled that fingerprints may be taken in connection with employment. *Miller v. NY Stock Exch.*, 306 F. Supp. 1002 (SDNY 1969) aff'd 452 F. 1074 (2d Cir. 1970) cert. den. 398 U.S. 905. The use of a conviction for crime as an *automatic* bar to private employment, however, may be an unconstitutional denial of due process. *Smith v. Fussenich*, 440 F. Supp. 1077 (D. Conn. 1977). In the case of the old New York police regulations for cabaret cards, however, a hearing was provided by which applicants could establish good character. If they still existed, the regulations might barely pass muster under contemporary law.

35. *Allegro*, December 1955, p. 6; January 1956, p. 1; "Music Moves Board" NYT, November 24, 1955, p. 39.

36. P. Benjamin, "City is Criticised on Cafe Licensing," NYT, May 10, 1961, p. 32; M. Gansberg, "15 'Village' Shops Ordered to Close," NYT, March 25, 1964, p. 43.

37. Max Gordon made this claim successfully in the thirties for the Village Vanguard: Gordon, Max, *Live at the Village Vanguard* (New York: DaCapo, 1982) p. 25. For the coffeehouses, see "Poetic License Needed," NYT, June 8, 1959, p. 54; "Judge Rules a Cafe, No Levy Must Pay, for Poetry Per Se," NYT, March 25, 1964, p. 43.

38. Conversation with Stefan Bauer-Mengelberg, May 22, 1990.

39. *People v. Ziegler*, 214 NYS 2d 177, 183 (Mag. Ct. 1961). cf. *People v. Rickoff*, 221 NYS 2d 116 (Mag. Ct. 1961). Curiously, there seems to have been a fight at the Figaro in 1965, at which no one was seriously hurt; Village leaders made use of it in their campaign to close coffeehouses. M. Gansberg, " 'Village' Chiefs Decry Violence," NYT, March 29, 1965, p. 35.

40. A. Clark, "Cafe Gift Charge Studied by Police," NYT April 6, 1961, p. 20; A. Clark, "Police Open Inquiry on Cafe Payoffs," April 7, 1961, p. 1; A. Clark, "30 More to Testify in Inquiry on Cafes," NYT, April 8, 1961, p. 1.

41. The three-musician rule is Local Law 92/1961 codified as NYC Admin. Code section B32-296, later recodified as 20-359. Coffeehouse licensing is Local Law 95/1961, codified as NYC Admin. Code section B32-310; "Coffee-house Bill Goes to Council,"NYT, November 29, 1961, p. 43; "Mayor Signs on $1.50 Base Pay," NYT, December 30, 1961, p. 20.

42. For Carol Greitzer, see E. Perlmutter, "A Liquor Ban in Parks is Urged to Halt Washington Sq. Decline," NYT, September 30, 1964, p. 45; H. Raymont, "Recreation Strip Sought in Village," NYT, July 17, 1966, p. 56; M. Carroll, "Many Cafes Here Called Illegal," NYT, June 13, 1969, p. 38. For Edward Koch and the coffeehouses, see, e.g. T. Buckley, "Civic Aide Linked to Coffeehouses," NYT, November 6, 1964, p. 29; H. Bigart, "Mayor Aids Drive on 'Village' Cafes" NYT, April 3, 1965, p. 31; H. Raymont, "Summonses Given to 2 Coffeehouses," NYT, September 18, 1966, p. 17; J. Kifner, " 'Village' Coffeehouse District Bustles the After Cleanup Order," NYT, December 28, 1967, p. 33.

43. L. Cooper, "Offices to Usurp 'Swing Row' Sites," NYT, August 2, 1953, section 8, p. 1; "52nd St. Club Raided" NYT, August 4, 1953, p. 15; "License Suspended for 3 Deuces Club," NYT August 8, 1953, p. 14.

44. Conversation with Joseph Termini, July 30, 1990; G. Giddins, "The Five Spot Closes. Highs and Lows of a Great Jazz Club," *Village Voice* February 16, 1976, p. 16.

45. Conversation with Robert Bookman, May 15, 1990.

46. G. Giddins, *op. cit.*

47. P. Dougherty, "Now the Latest Craze is 1-2-3 All Fall Down," NYT, February 11, 1965, p. 43 (discos); H. Rubenstein, "Diary of a Mad Nightclub Owner," *Egg*, April, 1990, p. 12.

48. N. Sheppard, "Consumer Agency Fears Budget Cuts," NYT, May 30, 1974, p. 29; F. Cerra, "Consumer Agency Fears Budget Cuts Drain Power," NYT, January 23, 1975, p. 37.

49. Conversation with Phil Schaap, May 30, 1990.

50. Local Law 41/1978.

51. W. Carr, "Cabaret Cards and the Cops," *New York Post* November 25, 1960, p. 50; "Civic Group Backs Cabaret Card Plan," NYT December 12, 1960, p. 37; Response to Freedom of Information request to NYC Department of Consumer Affairs, March 13, 1986.

Notes to Chapter 5

1. NYC Admin Code Section 20-105; Conversation with Peter Lempin, September 26, 1990.

2. The practice was condemned in *Charlotte's Fancy Rest. v. NYC*, 505 NYS 2d 615 (App. Div. 1 Dept. 1986), rev'd on other grounds 514 NYS 2d 714 (Ct. App. 1987). Description of the change in DCA policy is drawn from confidential sources.

3. J. Pareles, "At Unlicensed Jazz Clubs, 3 Is a Crowd, but 4 Is Illegal," *NYT*, March 19, 1987, p. B1, quotes justifications given by Consumer Affairs, including fire safety. The extra requirements were imposed by NYC Local Law 41 of 1978, called the "Blue Angel law." There is, however, nothing in the record of the Blue Angel fire to sustain the law's "focus of attention" argument. *Ripples of Clearview, Inc. v. Fruchtman*, Sup. Ct. NY. Co. No. 00846/80, an unsuccessful case attacking the added requirements, in which the City, as defendant, set forth the history of Local Law 41, discloses nothing in the Grand Jury report or elsewhere to support the theory. Nevertheless, the requirements were and are presumably in effect and enforceable.

4. Conversation with David Levy, June 18, 1990; with Junior Mance, June 4, 1990.

5. J. Pareles, "City Forces Clubs to Restrict Jazz", *NYT,* April 10, 1986, p. C13; conversation with Barry Harris, June 17, 1990.

6. Conversation with Mel Litoff, June 18, 1990; S. Troup, "Sour Notes: New Notes of Discord Hit the Business of Manhattan Clubs," *Newsday*, February 23, 1987, Part III, p.1.

7. J. Pareles, *op. cit.*, note 5.

8. S. Troup, *op. cit.*, note 6.

9. M. Johnson, "Protest City Council's Foot-Dragging on Messinger Amendment," *Amsterdam News*, March 23, 1985, p. 25.

10. Interview with James Robert Belden, May 29, 1990.

11. A. Krebs & R. Thomas, "From Bach to Pop in Hotel's Move to Change Image," *NYT*, April 13, 1981, p. 37.

12. Conversation with Ruth Messinger, August 7, 1990.

13. Conversation with Judy West, November 14, 1990.

14. S. Freedman, "Musicians Taking City Cabaret Law to Court." NYT, June 4, 1986, p. A2. For Ms. Greitzer's earlier career, see Chapt. 4, *supra*.

15. Letter of J. Glasel to C. Greitzer, September 19, 1984, Local 802 files; affidavit of John Glasel, *Chiasson* record, May 1, 1986. In a letter to *Crain's New York Business*, August 11, 1986, p. 10, Ms. Greitzer denied that Glasel helped to draft the bill.

16. I. Wilkerson, "Panel Hears Tuneful Protest of Limits on Music in Clubs" NYT, June 29, 1985, p. C15.

17. NYC Admin Code Section 24-241.1.

18. Affidavit of Julius Spector, *Chiasson* record, June 5, 1986.

19. These are, respectively, C4, C6, C7, C8 and M districts. NYC *Zoning Resolution* (ZR); NYC Dept. of City Planning, *Zoning Handbook* (1988). It was possible to become eligible for a license by special permit from the Board of Standards and Appeals in a C2 district, slightly less local than a C1 district. NYC *Zoning Resolution* Section 73-241. This created a double-licensing system, more fully explained in Chapter Seven.

20. "Cabaret Faces Zoning Court Test," *NYT*, January 22, 1967, Section 8, p. 1. It was, in fact, remarkable that the restaurant had been able to get a variance, which is supposed to be granted only when physical conditions on a lot give rise to a situation where strict compliance with zoning would lead to hardship and make the property unprofitable. ZR section 72-21. It was hard to see how Max's Kansas City fit this description.

21. Baumgartner, M.P., *Moral Order of A Subrub* (New York: Oxford, 1988); Sally Merry, "Mending Walls and Building Fences," paper presented at Law & Soc'y Meeting, Berkeley, CA, June, 1990.

22. Gans, Herbert, *The Levittowners* (New York: Pantheon, 1967).

23. Jacobs, Jane, *Death and Life of Great American Cities* (New York: Random House, 1961), pp. 16–25.

24. Whyte, W.H., *The City: Rediscovering The Center* (New York: Doubleday, 1988) pp. 6–7.

25. Interview with Fred Kent, June 12, 1990.

26. Jacobs. *op. cit.* Chapters 2, 7, 8.

27. "New York City Zoning: The Need for Reform" (New York: Nat. Res. Def. Council & Womens City Club, 1989) p. 8; Sennett, R., *Fall of Public Man* (New York: Vintage, 1978), pp. 12–16.

28. W.H. Whyte, *op. cit.* Chapter 16.

29. For sidewalk cafes, D. Shipler, "Sidewalk Cafes Bloom Here Despite Soot and Noise," *NYT*, June 17, 1968, p. 41; M. Carroll, "Many Cafes Here Called Illegal" NYT, June 13, 1969, p. 38; G. Fowler, "Stricter Zoning Rules for City's Sidewalk Cafes Proposed," *NYT*, September 15, 1979, p. 23; G. Fowler, "Strict Sidewalk Cafe Law Backed" NYT, October 4, 1979, p. B9. For performers, Editorial, "Two Small Victories," *NYT*, August 30, 1966, p. 40; "Street Theater's Appeal as Big as All Outdoors," *NYT*, April 1977, p. B1.

30. Conversation with Fred Kent, June 12, 1990.

31. Sennett, *op. cit.* pp. 20–23.

32. Oldenburg, Ray, *The Great Good Place* (New York: Paragon House, 1989) p. 18.

33. Conversation with Richard Sennett, September 14, 1990.

34. NYC Local Law 15/1971.

35. Conversation with William H. Whyte, May 30, 1990.

36. P. Chevigny, "Life Isn't Always a Cabaret," *NY Law Journal* January 16, 1987, p. 6.

37. Affidavit of David Sheldon, May 20, 1986, *Chiasson* record.

38. Conversation with Barry Harris, June 17, 1990; NYC Small Retail Business Study Comm'n, "Final Report" (Mimeo 1986) with Dissenting Report.

39. M. Gross, "Party Seems to Be Over for Lower Manhattan Clubs" *NYT*, October 26, 1985, p. 1.

40. A. Narvaez, "Planning Control Shifts Focus of Charter Vote" NYT, September 26, 1975, p. 30.

41. C. Kaiser, "First New York City Charter in 14 Years in Effect in New York City," *NYT*, January 3, 1977, p. 1.

42. P. Goldberger, "Urban Renewal: Money's The Problem," *NYT*, September 27, 1975, p. 19.

43. NYC Charter, Chapter 70.

44. NYC Charter Chapter 8. Compare NYC Charter section 197-C with section 200. Under the 197-c procedure (ULURP), the Community Board was required to hold a hearing and make a recommendation within 60 days, following which City PLanning had 60 days to act. These time limits are missing for text changes under section 200. The Charter changes of 1990 do not change these provisions in any way relevant here.

45. NYS Environmental Conservation Law, 17 1/2 *McKinneys Consol. Laws of NY* Section 8-0109.

Notes to Chapter 6

1. *Hilton Intern. Co. v. NLRB*, 690 F. 2d 318 (2nd Cir. 1982). See discussion in Chapter Two.

2. Statement of John Glasel, June 3, 1986, Local 802 files.

3. The Supreme Court case is *Monroe v. Pape*, 365 U.S. 167 (1961). Nina Simone's case is *Simone v. Kennedy*, 26 Misc. 2d 748, 212 NYS 2d 838 (Sup. Ct. NY Co. 1961), discussed in Chapter Four. The question whether the card system would be valid under present day law is discussed in Chapter Four, note 34.

4. See, e.g., A. Chayes, "Role of The Judge in Public Law Litigation" 89 Harvard Law Review 1281 (1976): T. Eisenberg and S. Schwab, "Reality of Constitutional Tort Litigation" 72 Cornell Law Review 641 (1987).

5. *Rizzo v. Goode*, 423 U.S. 362 (1976).

6. 452 U.S. 61 (1981).

7. *Id.* at 72–73.

8. *Id.* at 678.

9. Affidavit of David Amram, April 25, 1986, *Chiasson* record.

10. *City of Watseka v. Ill. Pub. Action Council*, 796 F. 2d. 1547, 1552 (7th Cir. 1986) aff'd summ. 479 U.S. 1048 (1987).

11. Affidavit of Daniel Queen, May 14, 1986, *Chiasson* record.

12. Memorandum of Law in Support of Motion for Preliminary Injunction, *Chiasson* record.

13. *Dallas v. Stanglin*, 490 U.S. 19 (1989). The case concerned a rule prohibiting young teen-agers at a dance hall, a problem which could have been treated as one of reasonable municipal regulation, without fully engaging the question of the rights of the dancers. The majority of the Court, however, chose to decide that the plaintiffs had no substantial interest in freedom of association derived from meeting others to dance with them. The case does not concern the interest of self-expression in the dancing, a more subtle problem. It is hard to see how a right of self-expression in social dancing, assuming that there is such a right, could be clearly presented merely because the dancers were denied entrance to a public hall. Social dancing is apparently not a performance art; that is to say, the dancers do it for their own pleasure and not for an audience (a proposition that is not free from doubt). They would be able to get the same expressive value from a dance in a private home or a school as in a hall. In order to present the issue of self-expression clearly, it might be necessary to show that there is no place other than the public hall for the dancers to congregate.

14. *People v. Walter*, 431 NYS 2d 776 (Crim. Ct. 1980); *Kemo v. Long Beach*, 261 NYS 2d 922 (Sup. Ct. Nassau Co. 1965) (questioning constitutionality); *Kent's Lounge v. City of NY*, 478 NYS 2d 928 (2nd Dept. 1984); *Merco v. Guggenheimer*, 395 F. Supp. 1322 (SDNY 1975) (upholding).

15. *Elrod v. Burns*, 427 U.S. 347, 373 (1976).

16. J. Pareles, "City Forces Clubs to Restrict Jazz," *NYT*, April 10, 1986, p. A27; D. Levy, "New York Mistreats Jazz," *NYT*, April 12, 1986, p. A27; S. Freedman, "Musicians Taking Cabaret Law to Court," *NYT*, June 4, 1986, p. A1; Editorial, "New York's Ill-Tuned Cabaret Law" *NYT*, June 26, 1986, p. A22.

17. Affidavit of Julius Spector, June 5, 1986, *Chiasson* record.

18. *Chiasson v. NYC Dept. of Consumer Affair*, 505 NYS 2d 499, 504 (Sup. Ct. NY Co. 1986).

19. "A Cabaret Law and All That Jazz" *National Law Journal*, December 15, 1986, p. 63; J.S. Wilson, "Trio with Jack Walrath," *NYT*, December 4, 1986, p. C16.

20. J. Pareles, "At Unlicensed Jazz Clubs, 3 Is a Crowd, but 4 is Illegal," *NYT*, March 19, 1987, p. B1; *People v. Bradley Friedle,* Crim. Ct. NY Co. No. 7N9900052 (Opinion April 30, 1987) (Cajun); Conversation with George Simon, June 18, 1980; Conversation with Paul Moore, July 24, 1986; June 11,

1990 (Sutton's); *Nolmar Rest. v. NYCDCA*, Sup. Ct. NY Co. 1987 (Freddy's); S. Troup. "Two More Jazz Rooms Suspend Performances," *Newsday*, January 28, 1987, Part II, p. 17.; S. Rosenthal, "Statute Clips Eagle's Wings," *New York Post*, June 19, 1987, p. 30; K. Johnson, "New York's Three-Musician Limit for Clubs is Held Unconstitutional" *NYT*, January 29, 1988, p. 1.

21. J. Pareles, *op. cit.* March 19, 1987; S. Rosenthal, "Cabaret's Catch-22" *New York Post*, July 6, 1987, p. 27; Affidavit of Mike Mikell, April 16, 1987, *Chiasson* record.

22. J. Pareles, *op. cit.* March 19, 1987; *New Yorker*, April 6, 1987, p. 8; Eric Pooley, "Sounds of The City," *New York*, May 4, 1987, p. 70. See also notes 20–21.

23. S. Troup, "Two More Jazz Rooms Suspend Performance," *Newsday*, January 28, 1987, Part II p. 17; S. Troup, "Sour Notes: New Notes of Discord Hit the Businesses of Manhattan Clubs" *Newday*, February 23, 1987, Part III p. 1.

24. Conversation with Andy Lugris (Visiones), June 1990; Felice Kirby (Teddy's) May 23, 1990; Michael Dorf, June 1990.

25. The following eight paragraphs based on materials from *Chiasson* record, as follows: Affidavits of: Michael Cuscuna, April 29, 1987; John Pareles, April 30, 1987; Jack Walrath, April 27, 1987; Mark Morganelli, April 29, 1987; John Glasel, April 29, 1987; Tony Trischka, April 30, 1987; Mike Mikell, April 16, 1987; Terry Pender, April 21, 1987.

26. 475 U.S. 41 (1986). There is a hole in the argument used by the Court here. The proof the Court allows will show a correlation between neighborhood decay and uses such as sexually explicit entertainment. The causation, however, remains obscure; the uses may gravitate to bad neighborhoods, for example, because of low rents. The correlation is nevertheless allowed as proof.

27. *City of Watseka v. Ill. Pub. Action Comm.*, 796 F. 2d 1547, 1555 fn. 15 (7th Circ. 1988) aff'd 479 U.S. 1048 (1987). To the same effect are *754 Orange Ave. v. West Haven*, 761 F. 2d 105 (2nd Cir. 1985); *Keego Harbor v. City of Keego Harbor*, 657 F. 2d 94, (6th Cir. 1981); *Tovar v. Billmeyer*, 721 F.2d 1260 (9 Cir. 1983) cert. den. 469 U.S. 872 (1984); *Kuzinich v. Sta. Clara Co.*, 689 F. 2d 1345 (9th Cir. 1983).

28. Affidavit of Brian Ketcham, April 27, 1987, *Chiasson* record.

29. D. Dunlap, "Clubs Shatter Peace of Gramercy Park," *NYT*, June 20, 1986, p. 35.

30. D. Levy, "New York City's Cabaret Law is Pulling The Plug On Jazz," *NYT*, April 3, 1987, p. A31; Editorial, "The Cabaret Law, Out of Tune," *NYT*, May 2, 1987, p. A26; see also S. Rosenthal, "Cabaret's Catch-22," *New York Post*, July 26, 1987, p. 27.

31. S. Troup, "Discord over Law That Sets Musician Limit," *Newsday*, May 13, 1987, p. 19.

32. This and the next quotation respectively are from *Chiasson v. NYC Dept. Consumer Affairs*, 524 NYS 2d 649, 651, 652 (Sup. Ct. NY Co. 1988).

33. This and following quotations from Justices David Saxe are from a conversation on September 28, 1990.

34. *Landsdown Entertainment v. NY Dept. Consumer Affairs*, 506 NYS 2d 825 (Sup. Ct. NY Co. 1986) aff'd 530 NYS 2d 574 (app. Div. 1st Dept 1988) aff'd 545 NYS 2d 82 (Ct. App. 1989).

35. *Seawall Assoc. v. City of NY*, 510 NYS 2d 435 (Sup. Ct. NY Co. 1986); 523 NYS 2d 353 (Sup. Ct. NY Co. 1987) rev'd 534 NYS 2d 958 (App. Div. 1st Dept. 1988) rev'd 544 NYS 2d 542 (Ct. App. 1989).

Notes to Chapter 7

1. NY Civil Prac. Law & Rules Sections 2219 (order); 5519 (stay).

2. *Board of Estimate v. Morris*, 489 US, 103 L.Ed. 2d 717 (1989).

3. Chip Deffaa, "Play All That Jazz," Bob Harrington, "Cabaret, Comedy Clubs Popping Corks" *New York Post*, January 29, 1988, p. 30; F. McMorris and P. O'Haire, "New Cabaret, Old Chum" NY *Daily News* January 29, 1988, p. 3; K. Johnson, "New York Three-Musician Limit for Clubs Is Held Unconstitutional," *NYT*, January 29, 1988, p. 1; J. Pareles, "Cabarets Celebrate End of Painful 'Prohibition' " *NYT*, February 1, 1988, p. B1; See also, S. Troup, "Ruling is Sweet Music for Clubs" *Newsday*, January 29, 88, p. 7; Editorial, "Let the Music Play" *NYT*, February 8, 1988, p. A18.

4. NY *Daily News*, January 29, 1988, p. 42.

5. Horowitz, Donald, *The Courts and Social Policy* (Washington DC: Brookings Institute, 1977). Judicial "activism" comes in at least two forms. One is practical, envisioning the judge intervening to run an organization, in an attempt to solve its problems. See e.g. Howard, J.W., *Courts of Appeals* (Princeton: Princeton University Press, 1981) Chapter 6. The other sort of activism is doctrinal, in which the judge pushes the limits of definitions of rights in such a way as to create legal innovation. Arguably neither of these is involved in the *Chiasson* decision.

6. Salins, Peter, ed, *New York Unbound* (New York: Blackwell, 1988) especially H. Hochman, "Clearing the Regulatory Clutter," pp. 93–108.

7. S. Troup, "Ruling Is Sweet Music for Clubs," *Newsday*, January 29, 1988, p. 7; Conversations with Judy Barnett, June 18, 1990; with Robert Appell of the Knitting Factory, May 14, 1990; with Andy Lugris, June 1990.

8. S. Troup, "Two More Jazz Rooms Suspend Performances" *Newsday*, January 28, 1987, Part II p. 17; Chip Deffaa, "Play All That Jazz" *New York Post*, January 29, 1988, p. 30; J. Pareles, "Cabarets Celebrate End of Painful 'Prohibition,' " *NYT*, February 1, 1988, p. B1.

9. P. Watrous, "Jazz for Dessert in Club Restaurants Where Music Is on the Menu," *NYT*, September 9, 1988, p. C1; K. Schoemer, "In Rocking East Village, The Beat Never Stops," *NYT*, June 8, 1990, p. C1.

10. T. Morgan, "Brooklyn Restaurants Going Live With The Sound of Music," *NYT*, October 17, 1988, p. B3.

11. "Sounds Around Town," *NYT*, May 25, 1990, p. C14; Interview with Joel Forrester, May 23, 1990; P. Watrous, "New York Home for Soviet Jazz," *NYT*, May 26, 1990, p. 12. The term "two-fisted piano" refers to an approach to the instrument different from that of, for example, Bud Powell, who did most of the melodic work with the right hand, and used the left primarily for rhythmic accents.

12. Some senior members of the Council dismissed the provisions about zoning with the formula, "the Council has no power to legislate on zoning; that's up to City Planning and the Board of Estimate." Although the Board of Estimate and the Commission did have authority over the uses of city land, including the power to draw up the Zoning Resolution, I could find nothing in the Charter or anywhere else that said the City Council could not pass legislation providing some limits in the interest of the general welfare. According to sources at the Charter Revision Commission, the Board of Estimate apparently had exclusive power over land-use legislation before 1931, when the City Council was created and the powers of the Board of Estimate were limited. Following this change, it appears that the Council did have power to legislate on land-use. Indeed, a provision of the Charter of 1931, section 39, said that a local law had to be submitted for a referendum if it "curtails the powers of the City Planning Commission." Thus, City officials were following customs of deferring to the Mayor and the Board of Estimate that were more than half a century old, and arguably no longer in effect. In any arena of regulation where land-use overlapped with any other municipal endeavor, then, the power to bring about change was effectively ceded to the mayor's office, because nobody else could coordinate all the efforts.

These legal details are now principally of historical interest, since the Charter revision of 1990 which abolished the Board of Estimate.

13. City Planning News, "Changes in Entertainment Use Regulations Proposed" April 17, 1989; City Planning Commission proposal of June 21, 1989. There were also proposals, later dropped, for limiting hours in discos and larger clubs, as well as added safety requirements. Under City Environmental Quality Review, officials found that the plan would "not result in significant adverse air quality or noise impacts. . . ." CEQR#89-252Y, April 17, 1989.

14. NYC Charter §200; *Zoning Res.* Section 73-241; *Zoning Handbook* (1988) pp. 98–101.

15. *Matter of West 79th Street 'Museum' Block Assoc. v. BSA* (Sup. Ct. NY Co.) No. 19341/89. (Lebedeff, J.); Conversation with Robert Bookman, May, 15, 1990; with Norman Marcus, May 25, 1990.

16. Conversation with Mel Litoff, June 18, 1990. There may be other examples, of which I have no personal knowledge.

17. Conversation with Norman Marcus, May 25, 1990.

18. P. Goldberger, "Shaping The Face of New York" in Salins, P., ed. *New York Unbound* (New York: Blackwell, 1988) pp. 127–140.

19. Kayden, Jerold, *Incentive Zoning in New York City: A Cost-Benefit Analysis* (Lincoln Inst. of Land Policy, 1978); Nat. Res. Def. Council and Womens

City Club, *NYC Zoning: The Need for Reform* (1989) pp. 7–9; Whyte, William H., *The City: Rediscovering The Center* (New York: Doubleday, 1988) Chapter 16.

20. S. Troup, "Sour Notes: New Notes of Discord Hit the Business of Manhattan Clubs," Newsday, February 23, 1987, Part III p. 1; Conversation with Paul Moore, June 11, 1990; Conversation with Michael Dorf, June 1990.

21. Manhattan Borough Board Resolution of June 15, 1989.

22. Statement of David Sheldon, Board of Estimate, October 23, 1989.

23. Conversation with Barbara Fife, July 24, 1990.

Notes to Chapter 8

1. Conversation with Phil Schaap, May 30, 1990.

2. Conversation with Peter Watrous, June 8, 1990.

3. Conversation with Phil Schaap, May 30, 1990.

4. Conversation with Barry Harris, June 17, 1990; with Henry Threadgill, June 17, 1990.

5. Conversation with Sonny Fortune, June 11, 1990; "Sounds Around Town" *NYT*, June 8, 1990, p. C22.

6. Conversation with Warren Chiasson, June 6, 1990.

7. S. Holden, "The Pop Life," *NYT*, May 30, 1990, p. C16.

8. Conversation with Peter Bernstein, May 29, 1990; with Carol Britto, May 29, 1990.

9. P. Watrous, "Pop/Jazz: Bill Frisell's Progress in Music's Avant-Garde" *NYT*, May 25, 1990, C14.

10. Conversation with Arnie Lawrence, June 6, 1990; with Peter Bernstein, March 29, 1990.

11. *Jazz Beat*, August 1988, p. 1.

12. S. Troup, "A Creative Quintet" *Newsday*, March 16, 1988, Part II p. 8; S. Troup, "On Music: Sound Advice" *Newsday*, August 11, 1989, Weekend Section p. 15.

13. Conversation with Bobby Sanabria, June 1990.

14. Conversation with James Robert Belden, May 16, 1990; May 26, 1990.

15. See, e.g., T. Sancton, "Horns of Plenty" *Time*, October 22, 1990, p. 64; Tom Piazza, "Young, Gifted and Cool," *NYT Magazine*, May 20, 1990, p. 34.

16. Benjamin, W. "The Work of Art in the Age of Mechanical Reproduction" in *Illuminations*, (New York: Schocken, 1969) pp. 217–251.

17. Conversation with Bobby Sanabria, June 1990.

18. Conversation with Joel Forrester, May 23, 1990.

Notes to Chapter 9

1. A. Giordano, "Killing a Dream," *Valley Advocate* (Springfield, MA) August 13, 1990, p. 1.

2. NYC City Council Resolution No. 673, December 9, 1986.

3. J. Pareles, "At Unlicensed Jazz Clubs, 3 Is a Crowd but 4 Is Illegal," *NYT*, March 19, 1987, p. B1.

4. P. Goldberger, "Shaping The Face of New York" in Salins, Peter, ed., *New York Unbound* (New York: Blackwell, 1988) p. 129.

5. Burger, P., *Theory of The Avant Garde* (Minneapolis: University of Minnesota, 1984) Chapter 3.

6. Rheinstein, M., ed., *Max Weber on Law in Economy and Society* (New York: Simon & Schuster, 1967) Chapters VI, XI.

7. P. Bourdieu, "The Force of Law: Toward A Sociology of the Juridical Field" 38 *Hastings Law Journal* 201, 246 (1987).

8. Foucault, M., *Power/Knowledge* (New York: Pantheon, 1984) Chapter 5.

INDEX